Human Services and Long-term Care

Providing human service through markets is inherently problematic. Quality care is critical, and unsatisfactory human service greatly influences people's quality of life. Yet, profit for human service providers is essential for sustainable service provision. This book focuses on striking a balance between human services' need for quality assurance and market providers' need for profit.

Yoshihiko Kadoya is Director of the Hiroshima Institute of Health Economics Research (HiHER) and Associate Professor of Economics, Hiroshima University, Japan.

T0371719

Routledge Studies in the Modern World Economy

For a full list of titles in this series, please visit www.routledge.com/series/SE0432

Human Services and Long-term Care
A Market Model

Yoshihiko Kadoya

Routledge
Taylor & Francis Group

LONDON AND NEW YORK

First published 2018
by Routledge
2 Park Square, Milton Park, Abingdon, Oxon OX14 4RN

and by Routledge
605 Third Avenue, New York, NY 10017

First issued in paperback 2020

Routledge is an imprint of the Taylor & Francis Group, an informa business

British Library Cataloguing-in-Publication Data
A catalogue record for this book is available from the British Library

Library of Congress Cataloging-in-Publication Data
Names: Kadoya, Yoshihiko, author.
Title: Human services and long-term care : a market model /
   by Yoshihiko Kadoya.
Description: Abingdon, Oxon ; New York, NY : Routledge, 2018. |
   Series: Routledge studies in the modern world economy ; 175 |
   Includes bibliographical references and index.
Identifiers: LCCN 2017054686 | ISBN 9781138630932 (hardback) |
   ISBN 9781315209159 (ebook)
Subjects: LCSH: Older people—Long-term care. | Older people—
   Services for. | Human services. | Caregivers.
Classification: LCC RA564.8 .K33 2018 | DDC 362.16—dc23
LC record available at https://lccn.loc.gov/2017054686

ISBN 13: 978-0-367-50424-3 (pbk)
ISBN 13: 978-1-138-63093-2 (hbk)

Typeset in Galliard
by Apex CoVantage, LLC

Contents

Figures

Tables

Preface

This book, *Human Services and Long-term Care: A Market Model,* is not a summary of existing economic research on the long-term care market. Rather, it makes the point that there is no existing economic model that is suitable to solve the problems in the human service market, including the long-term care market. In addition, this book proposes a mechanism suitable for ensuring both efficiency and quality, which has long been a problem in the human service market, from an interdisciplinary point of view as well as an economic perspective.

In summary, this book aims to transition from a model in which existing prices and quality are the selection factors for long-term care services, to a model that excludes price and in which quality alone is the selection factor. In the conventional model in which price and quality are the selection factors, a wide range of goods is created, from those that are "high quality but expensive" to those that are "low quality but inexpensive." This "market image" is not a problem in the case of general goods, such as daily necessities, but it is not suitable for a market like human services, in which poor quality goods can significantly lower the user's quality of life. This is because while the market image is not a problem for the wealthy, the economically vulnerable can find their quality of life significantly lowered by the long-term care they receive, which contradicts the original spirit and meaning of human services. In Chapter 2 of this book, a proposed "care market model (CMM)" is presented, and all subsequent chapters are based on this proposed model.

The origin of the problem of low-quality services that the human service market has faced for many years is that discussion about market design has taken place separately in each of the respective fields. In other words, the debate about the form that the growth of human services should take, the proposed market to provide such services, and the verification thereof has not taken place in an integrated manner. To borrow the words of *The Oxford Handbook of Welfare States,* a comprehensive handbook of welfare policy research published in 2010 by 5 editors and more than 70 authors, and also Nishimura (2014), in each of their respective fields, sociologists are strongly interested in social integration, economists in economic efficiency, political scientists in conflict between social hierarchies, and researchers of social policy in the redistribution of wealth to the poor and emergency measures to improve poverty. There has been a noticeable lack of an integrated discussion that transcends the boundaries of each of these fields. From this viewpoint, this book attempts to provide a proposal from a three-dimensional perspective while also giving consideration to each of these fields.

As described above, the aim of this book is ambitious. It points out the following weakness: that the depth of the field in itself can become a trap, and there is a danger that the discussion becomes too shallow when considered from the viewpoint of each field. I hope that the content of this book is discussed and further refined by readers in many fields.

For this book, I modified and added to my doctoral dissertation *Managing the Human Service Market: The Case of Long-Term Care in Japan,* submitted to the University of Sydney in April 2011. I received extremely valuable feedback from a very large number of people for this book, and while I am not able to thank them all here, I would particularly like to express my gratitude to the following people for their guidance; Associate Professor Joanne Kelly, Associate Professor Gaby Ramia, Professor Geoff Gallop, and Professor Gabriele Meagher (all from the University of Sydney), Professor Paul Posner (George Mason University), Professor Emeritus Seiritsu Ogura, (Hosei University), Associate Professor Karen Hayashida (University of Hawaii), Professor Emeritus Shuzo Nishimura (Kyoto University), Professor Charles Yuji Horioka (Asian Grouth Institute), Professor Eiji Mangyo (Nagoya University), Professor Kenji Mizutani (Nagoya University), Dr. Nopphol Witvorapong (Chulalongkorn University), and Dr. Mostafa Saidur Rahim Khan (Hiroshima University).

Among the chapters, a modified version of Chapter 4 was previously published in the *Japanese Journal of Health Economics and Policy,* and I received many valuable suggestions from the anonymous peer reviewers. In addition, the content of this book formed the basis for a presentation I gave in 2013 by invitation of the United States branch of the Japan Society for the Promotion of Science, another lecture in 2014 by invitation from the National Health Security Office, Government of Thailand, and keynote speech in 2017 by invitation from Mae Fah Luang University, Thailand. The manuscript, published as *Kaigo shijo no keizaigaku* in Japanese, received the best authorship award of the Public Policy Studies Association Japan 2017.

This work was supported by the JSPS KAKENHI [grant number 15K17075], [grant number 15KK0083], and RISTEX, JST.

I thank both Ms. Samantha Phua and Ms. Yongling Lam from Routledge for their patience and valuable suggestions throughout the publication process.

Any errors in the content of this book are wholly my responsibility.

Last but not least, I would like to thank my wife Nutchanart and our 3-year-old daughter for their selfless and constant support.

Introduction

The human service age and new economics

Providing human services through competitive markets is inherently problematic (Donabedian, 1987; Hansmann, 1980; Lipsky, 1980; Nyman, 1994; Wiener *et al.*, 2007). On one hand, governments in the Organisation for Economic Co-operation and Development (OECD) member nations cannot afford to respond to today's human service needs. The government bureaucratic model that led to an adherence to prescribed procedures has proved unsustainable, because human services need to be flexible to respond to rapid changes in society (Thomas, 2006). In this context, the non-government sector is more flexible and specialized in the service field. Nonetheless, human service provision through competitive markets tends to leave users vulnerable to the profit-driven whims of private-sector providers, particularly those "weaker" users lacking in financial means. Unlike the choices of goods, like cups and bowls in markets in which differences in quality will not have a major impact on the quality of life, the choice of human services, such as nursing homes, disability long-term care institutes, and child-care centers, has an enormous influence on peoples' quality of life. An extreme example is that in recent decades, a great number of elderly people have suffered from long-term care of inappropriate quality, and in some cases actual abuse, in the competitive markets of long-term care in many countries, including Japan (OECD, 2005). People should have the right to lead "maintain the minimum standards of wholesome and cultured living" (Article 25, The Constitution of Japan). Social security is a system to ensure that that state provides its citizens with the minimum standard of living (the so-called "national minimum"). It is unacceptable to place some users in a position of being weaker in the provision of human services that constitute part of this system, even if, for example, the provision of such services through competitive markets is essential.

From this viewpoint, this book examines the provision of human services through competitive markets as an example of long-term care for the elderly. Specifically, the following two questions are dealt with.

1   How should governments design the human service market to ensure services of a certain level of quality?
2   How should the indicators to measure the quality of the services provided be set?

The analysis mainly used the cases of several OECD members, but the primary focus is Japan, which has the highest demand for such care provision per capita, and which, in fact, leads the world in the design of the human service market.

This book is divided into two parts. Part I reveals the weaknesses by which some providers can sacrifice the quality of care for market competition. The research then presents an alternative, the care market model (CMM), which aims to direct market competition to enhance the quality of long-term care. Next, the model presented is validated. Then, it is clarified that while some hypotheses appear to conflict with the model, in fact, the model is not inconsistent with them.

Part II presents a process-based performance measurement as an indicator of human service quality, proposing a modification to the public policy model of recent years, which is committed to utilizing market principles. The research clarifies that the problem of low-quality long-term care has continued, because the current mainstream outcome-based performance measurement, which focuses on outcomes, is not suitable. More specifically, the research points out that outcome-based indicators that require clear targets conflict with the ambiguous policy goals of human services. Finally, the research attempts to modify the existing model to use process-based measurement.

Two propositions recur throughout the analysis and findings presented in this study.

1   Governments need to implement a long-term care market model to direct market competition to enhance the quality of services.
2   Governments need to develop a process-based performance measurement that focuses on the service process.

From these prepositions, three main arguments follow. First, governments need to strike a balance between market contestability and service quality assurance. On the one hand, market contestability is necessary for sustainable human service provision, because it promotes the necessary innovation and flexibility. On the other hand, market contestability accommodates inexpensive but low-quality long-term care in the market. Governments are required to eliminate inexpensive but low-quality long-term care, which leads to neglect and abuse, and to direct the contestability for the positive sides of the market. Second, governments need to introduce systems to provide users with service quality information about providers. In human service markets, users normally cannot choose a provider based on its service quality, because there is information asymmetry between users and providers. Third, governments need to develop process-based performance measurement for human services; governments should not rely on outcome-based performance measurement. The policy goals of human services, such as a peaceful life in old age, are ambiguous and therefore, notoriously difficult to be measured in a meaningful way (Lipsky, 1980).

The problem of human service provision through competitive markets originates from the contradiction between the essential mission of human services and the nature of markets. Since human services are aimed at guaranteeing the basic developmental and long-term care needs of *people*, human service provision needs strong government ethics; that is, it is essential to ensure at least some minimum level of service for everyone and avoid poor service for anyone. However, the fundamental nature of competitive markets is that while they create expensive but high quality long-term care services, they allow inexpensive but poor quality long-term care services to exist. Suppose q indicates quality and p price. The provided services in competitive markets can be expressed as $\Upsilon = x\,(q,\,p)$. In this formula, the market allows the co-existence of a wide range of quality, from very good to very poor. This range may be acceptable in consumer items, but not in human services.

Up to the present, many governments have tried to eliminate poor quality services by implementing regulatory policies; for example, they have imposed minimum requirements for service providers, such as ratios for care workers to long-term care recipients, complaint offices, and emergency access to hospitals, and can suspend the businesses of providers who do not meet the regulations.

However, low-quality long-term care remains, including from providers who neglect and abuse users. However, in the first place, prior to eliminating low-quality long-term care, it is very difficult to identify these types of human services, as there is no absolute single measurement of human service quality (Donabedian, 1987). Moreover, what to measure varies according to the time. In the long-term care market, for instance, physical abuse by caregivers would have been a unique signal to disqualify care several decades ago but would no longer be sufficient today. Mental abuse by caregivers must also be recognized, because required care has continuously been changing.

Governments need to strike a balance between the mission of human services and the nature of competitive markets, but a suitable market model and service performance measurement have not yet been established. This is the source of the problem of human service provision through competitive markets.

Why investigate the case of long-term care for the elderly?

The case of long-term care for the elderly (hereafter, "long-term care") provides an excellent opportunity to undertake a systemic analysis of this problem for three reasons. First, most OECD nations have chosen to provide long-term care through competitive markets in order to respond to increasing needs. Long-term care has already occupied the biggest number of users of human services in almost all OECD nations, and this trend will continue to grow in the next decades.

Second, in long-term care, from the viewpoint of a national minimum, governments are strongly required by moral imperatives to ensure a certain level of service in the market. Frail elderly, especially those who suffer from cognitive problems, often cannot exercise their consumer rights by leaving and complaining about low-quality long-term care, owing to physical and mental constraints.

Table 0.1 The speed of the shift from aging to aged society in East Asian nations

	Reached year of aging society: share of older people (Aged 65+) in the population is 7% or More	Reached year of aged society: share of older people (aged 65+) in the population is 14% or more	Elapsed years
Hong Kong	1983	2014	31 years
Taiwan	1993	2018	25 years
Singapore	1999	2016	17 years
China	2002	2026	24 years
Thailand	2002	2024	22 years
Malaysia	2020	2043	23 years
Indonesia	2018	2039	21 years
More developed regions*	1950**	2000	50 years+
OECD average	– ***	2006	–

Source: United Nations (2008) and OECD (2009)

  * More developed regions, defined by the United Nations (2008), comprise all regions of Europe plus Northern America, Australia/New Zealand, and Japan.
 ** The ratio of older people in the population was already 7.9% in that year, but data prior to 1950 are not available.
*** The oldest information available is in 1970 (9.6%).

It is highly likely that the elderly will find themselves in this sort of situation in the last stage of life, and depending on the circumstances, this stage can continue from a few months to more than 10 years. The lessons learned from long-term care provision would seem to offer many suggestions for other fields of human services.

Third, the suggestions obtained from the research on long-term care will remain important for many decades at the very least. Today, the challenge of long-term care provision through competitive markets is faced only by advanced nations (i.e., OECD members), which are experiencing aging populations. However, many other nations are expected to deal with the same problem in the near future. For instance, the growth of aging populations in East Asia is much faster than that of OECD members. Table 0.1 indicates the shift from an aging society to an aged society in many East Asian nations – such as China, Hong Kong, Singapore, Taiwan, Malaysia, Indonesia, and Thailand – compared with developed nations.

Why study the case of Japan?

Although this book investigates various OECD member nations, the focus is on Japan. There are three main reasons. First, Japan is the front-runner of aging-population societies. As shown in Figure 0.1, Japan has the highest share of very old people in the population and it is expected to keep this position for

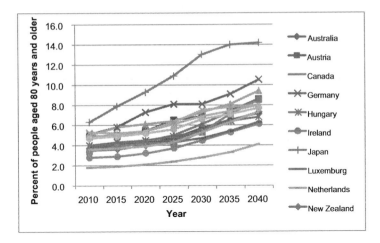

Figure 0.1 Share of very old people (aged 80+ years) in the populations of selected OECD members

Source: United Nations (2012)

Note: Most long-term care recipients belong to the age group of very old (aged 80 years and more) (OECD, 2005).

several decades. This means that Japan is not only facing the most pressing need in the world to cope with the problem of long-term care provision through a competitive market, but also that Japan's case is attracting attention from other countries around the world.

The second reason for selecting Japan is that, overall, it is dealing with this challenge very well. In fact, although the data are a little old, the expense of long-term care per capita in Japan is not high compared to the other OECD members (see Figure 1.2 in Chapter 1). This signifies that Japan efficiently utilizes the innovation and flexibility of a competitive market in long-term care provision. Moreover, according to comparative care quality-assurance research by Wiener *et al.* (2007: 5), long-term care in Japan is perceived as the least problematic in terms of care quality. This implies that the Japanese government to a certain extent successfully ensures the quality of care in a competitive market.

Third, practically no mention has been made of the long-term care market model in previous studies and despite the fact that Japan performs well in terms of human service (long-term care) provision through a competitive market, very little prior research has investigated the model provided by Japan. The majority of the prior research in this area concentrates on the United States.

Research design and methods

In studying how governments can strike a balance between the objectives of human service provisions and the nature of competitive markets, this research takes a model-testing approach. Specifically, Part I presents a new care market model, which I name the CMM, in order for governments to regulate market competition to enhance care quality. This research then tests the implementability, efficacy, and financial sustainability of CMM by primarily analyzing the case of the Japanese long-term care market. Part II of this book presents and tests a model, specifically, a process-based performance measurement model, and its applicability and financial sustainability is confirmed.

Given such multi-dimensional processes of testing that go beyond the framework of such fields as economics and public administration, the research inevitably combines diverse methods and both quantitative and qualitative approaches. An outline and summary of these methods is provided in each chapter.

Part I consists of five different methods. First, in order to investigate the applicability of CMM, this book seeks a market that meets the preconditions of CMM, by surveying OECD nations. Second, in finding a market that meets the preconditions, the research further investigates the market, using the case study method (Yin, 2002). Third, to test the efficacy of CMM, the research investigates models that conflict with the idea of CMM by regression analysis. The examination utilizes quantified care quality data, published by local governments of Japan, and testing variables of 1,093 group home providers. Investigating the correlation between the data and testing variables, the research analyzes the validity of the conflicting models and workability of CMM. Fourth, by testing the financial sustainability of CMM, the research again conducts a survey of OECD nations. Analyzing the financial information of these nations, the research establishes a condition for the sustainability of CMM. Fifth, as an additional argument, the research proposes the leverage model. This model is developed because it can be used for markets that do not qualify for the preconditions of CMM.

In Part II, the research also combines different methods. First, testing the applicability of the presenting process-based performance measurement model, the research compares the cases of Japan, which has applied the model, and the United States, which uses a different model. Second, to further test the efficacy and financial sustainability of the process-based performance measurement model, the research utilizes case analysis, focusing on the details of the Japanese case.

Defining the area of study

Although the definition of human services is changing (Schmolling *et al.*, 1997; Zins, 2001), the concept today is a synonym for or a part of social welfare services. Zins (2001: 6–7) defines human services as "institutionalized systematic services" aimed at "meeting human needs . . . required for maintaining or promoting the overall quality of life" of service users. The field of human services includes childcare, healthcare, long-term care, disability care, and family support. In fact, several governments are in charge of such services using the name "human service" (e.g., Department of Human Service, Government of Australia; Department of Health and Human Service, United States Government). This research specifically deals with the field of long-term care.

Long-term care brings together a variety of services for people who are dependent on help with basic activities of daily living (ADL) for extended periods. Such activities include bathing, dressing, eating, getting in and out of bed or on or off a chair, moving around, and using the bathroom. These long-term care needs are due to longstanding chronic conditions that cause physical or mental disability. As in many other previous studies on long-term care, this study distinguishes between long-term care services and medical services, such as interim hospitalization, medical diagnoses, and prescription drugs.

Although long-term care does not necessarily mean long-term care for older people, the categories are closely aligned. Certainly, the age of the care recipient is not an eligibility criterion for long-term care programs in most OECD member countries. Nevertheless, according to the OECD (2005: 25), "As a rule of thumb, around 80 percent of users of home-care services and some 90 percent of nursing home residents are aged 65 and older." For this reason, throughout this book, the terms "long-term care" and "long-term care for older people" are often used interchangeably.

Competitive markets that provide human services, which are an important area of study in this book, allow providers to compete with each other, but such competition is inevitably regulated. It is clear that a perfectly competitive market does not ensure the users a minimum standard, which is an important mission of human service provision. There are three levels of regulations on competition: competitive tendering and contracting (CTC), license subsidies (LS), and hybrids of CTC and LS. The definitions vary slightly according to the literature, but according to Davidson (2009), in CTC, government agencies choose the providers for a designated group of users, whereas in LS, entry is open for any provider that meets a set of minimum requirements (i.e., license). The hybrid is literally a mixture of CTC and LS.

The bigger the demand for human services is, the more competitors governments need to admit, because mass provision requires innovative and efficient aspects of competitive markets. In long-term care markets, most countries in the OECD, which are experiencing aging populations, have introduced a license subsidies system, and others are expected to follow their lead.

Chapter overview and arguments

As indicated at the beginning of this chapter, this book argues that in human service provision through competitive markets, governments need to ensure a certain quality of service. Three secondary arguments support this book: (a) governments need to strike a balance between market contestability and service quality assurance, (b) governments need to introduce a system to provide users with information about the providers' service quality, and (c) governments need to develop process-based performance measurement for human service provision.

Chapter 1 of this research is a broad survey of historical and theoretical work on human service provision through competitive markets. The chapter begins by outlining the reason that governments need to be responsible for human service provision. Tracing the origins of human service, the research investigates the changes in governments' commitments to human service provision. This includes a discussion on why, in today's democratic systems, governments are urged to ensure a certain standard of living by being responsible for human service provision. The chapter then provides an overview of how human services are provided through competitive markets and how governments have tried to ensure care quality, concluding that the challenges faced today converge on two points: (a) market models to direct market competition to enhance the quality of care, and (b) performance measurements to evaluate and regulate providers' quality of care.

Part I, which consists of Chapters 2, 3, 4, and 5, investigates the market design for long-term care provision. Since competitive markets facilitate the existence of poor quality care, this part examines how governments should modify the existing market model in order to eliminate such poor quality care. Specifically, the research focuses on directing market competition to enhance the quality of care, so that poor quality care is eliminated from the market.

Chapter 2 introduces the CMM presented in this research. Although the market model for human service provision through competitive markets is very important, prior research has not presented a market model that assumes the universal care system, which is applied in nearly half of OECD member countries. Most of this prior research has relied on easily obtainable data on the United States, which applies a means-tested care system. However, the market model developed in the United States has several crucial defects. First, Medicaid, the government funded means-tested program, does not allow care recipients to pay attention to care quality, because the reimbursement rate is independent of care needs. Second, because the model contains the component of price competition, poor quality care remains in the market. Furthermore, the efficacy of care quality regulations in the model is limited, because such regulations cause market price rises, which could deprive non-wealthy care recipients of access to care. Chapter 2, therefore, presents the CMM, which directs market competition solely for better quality care in order to get rid of poor quality care. This model requires three conditions: (a) a universal long-term care system, (b) standardized content of care according to care recipients' conditions, and (c) no price competition. The following three chapters investigate the CMM in terms of implementability, efficacy, and financial sustainability, respectively.

Chapter 3 examines the implementability of the CMM. Investigating the Japanese long-term care markets, the chapter shows that the market for group homes for the elderly with dementia (hereafter, group home) in Japan meets all conditions of the CMM. That is, in the group home market, standardized content of care according to levels of care required by the care recipients is provided with no price competition through competitive markets and within universal care.

Chapter 4 verifies the efficacy of the CMM. In the health economics literature, three models, based on information asymmetry between users and providers in care-related markets, conflict with the utility of the CMM. The conflicted models are as follows:

1   the contract failure model, which claims users perceive non-profit providers as a sign of good service quality (i.e., users cannot choose a provider solely based on its quality of care);
2   the medical arms race (MAR) model, which argues that competition in the care market tends to lower the service quality; and
3   Suzuki and Satake's (2001) model, which claims that new entrants in the care market do not contribute to improvement in the market's care quality.

Testing the three conflicted information asymmetry models, the research reveals that none of the three models was fully supported in the group home for the elderly with dementia market in Japan. As a result, it is possible for the CMM to direct market competition to enhance the market's quality of care. The findings of this chapter suggest that publishing providers' care quality evaluations should be added as a fourth condition to the CMM, initially set out in Chapter 3.

The first half of Chapter 5 examines the financial sustainability of the CMM. One may consider that the implementation of the CMM is costly for governments, because one of the CMM's conditions is to introduce a universal care system: care for "everyone," not just for the economically vulnerable. Nonetheless, an analysis of the correlation between public long-term care expenditure per share of very old people in populations and care systems indicates that the universal system does not necessarily cost more than a system of care solely for the economically vulnerable. The research further reveals that the size of the domestic economic gap greatly influences the financial efficiency of long-term care provision. That is, even if governments universally cover peoples' long-term care expenses, public expenditure remains comparatively small as long as the gap between rich and poor stays small.

The second half of Chapter 5 presents the model of care quality improvements using leverage as an alternative solution for governments that cannot immediately introduce a universal care system (i.e., governments of nations with bigger economic inequality gaps). Analyzing the correlations among care quality indicators, the model of care quality improvements using leverage finds that the leveraged indicator has the most positive influence on the other indicators, indicating that the indicator can be improved relatively easily. The quality of long-term care can be efficiently enhanced by using leverage and focusing resources on the indicator that can be easily improved.

As previously described, Part I proves that governments can direct market competition to enhance care quality by implementing the CMM, and thus, Part II investigates how to measure the quality of care, namely, performance measurement.

Chapter 6 provides an alternative care policy model (CPM) to the existing public policy model, and presents an alternative, process-based performance measurement. As Chapter 2 questions the current public policy model, Chapter 7 compares both outcome-based performance measurement and the alternative process-based performance measurement. The chapter finds weaknesses in both measurements. On the one hand, the process-based measurement does not fit the current public policy model and for a long time, has not been the focus of attention. On the other hand, the outcome-based measurement does fit the current public policy model, but it does not fit the ambiguous policy goals of human services. Favoring process-based performance measurement from the view of solving the care quality problem, the research presents the CPM to modify the current public policy model in order to accommodate the use of process-based performance measurement. Process-based performance measurement under CPM consists of evaluating the measures (i.e., the process of care implementation) and the training of care workers. The subsequent two chapters examine performance measurement in terms of the empirical validity of the measures and the training of care workers, respectively.

Chapter 7 investigates the measures for care workers in the presented process-based performance measurement under the CPM. To do so, this chapter specifically compares two cases: the Japanese long-term care market with the presented process-based measurement and the United States long-term care market with the existing outcome-based performance measurement. Analyzing two empirical cases, the chapter proves that the long-term care market produces better results when governments implement process-based performance measurement under the CPM.

Chapter 8 investigates the kind of training needed for process-based performance measurement. Among the OECD members, the United States and Japan appear as the only nations that require minimum training for care workers nationally. Analyzing the two nations clarifies that care workers' training mainly has two phases and that both are useful for ensuring quality of care. In other words, whereas Phase 1 standardizes the care quality of overt needs by ensuring proper care attitudes and physical skills (e.g., transfer techniques), Phase 2 enables care workers to respond to potential care needs by teaching workers to appreciate care recipients' mentalities and by training communication skills to pick up potential care recipients' needs. Therefore, Phase 2 training is preferred for the use of process-based performance measurement. Certainly, Phase 2 training is concerned about sustainability, as it requires more resources (time and cost). However, the research finds that by presenting a career path to Japan's care workers that utilizes their field knowledge and experience, it becomes easier to spread this field experience across long-term care policy as a whole, and moreover, it indicates the importance of a mechanism to ensure excellent care workers.

Chapter 9 considers a framework utilized in industrial policy for care needs drawn up from the training of care workers. Policies to ensure the sustainability of the CMM are examined, and their mechanism and sources of funding are discussed, alongside issues facing the long-term care market in Japan.

Chapter 10 summarizes the consideration of this book, of "Human Services and Long-Term Care: A Market Model" originating first from Japan. By reviewing the CMM and CPM presented in this book and arranging the arguments, this chapter presents the models as answers to the research questions of this book. Summarizing the research contributions, the chapter shapes the implications for the existing public policy model and, finally, describes remaining problems for future research.

1 Studying human service provision through competitive markets

Research on the human service market can be divided into studies on the efficacy of market provision of human services and studies on the negative consequences on quality of care. One view presents market utilization for human service provision as a necessary trend, arguing that governments today cannot afford direct provision of services owing to their technical and financial capacity limitations. Conversely, it has been frequently noted that such market utilization has caused significant damage to the quality of life of care receivers, because market competition tends to sacrifice quality for profit maximization (even, e.g., if only for one component of quality). In summary, the existing literature offers contradictory findings on the utility of providing human services through the market, providing evidence that further analysis is necessary.

This chapter reviews the existing literature and identifies areas of limitation. Whereas most research intends to adjust the nature of human services to the market, utilizing the current public policy model, there have been hardly any attempts to modify the current model to reflect the nature of human services. Certainly, market-oriented theories have been very useful in many other types of public service provision, in which public services provided through the market have successfully enhanced the efficiency of human service without loss of quality.[1] Thus, it was reasonable for researchers to suggest that the quality issue of human services could be solved by government regulatory policies. Nonetheless, such symptomatic treatment has not solved the issue for decades because the nature of human service is very different from that of other public services. This book, therefore, adjusts the current public policy model to accommodate the nature of human service provision.

The arguments presented in this chapter flow in the following order. First, the reasons for governments assuming initial responsibility for the provision of human services are reviewed, alongside how service providers have shifted from governments to markets. Furthermore, a rise of poor service quality and governments' efforts to solve it are explained, with a particular focus on long-term care. The cause of quality loss, which has continued for many years, is analyzed, and the fundamental disagreements between the market-utilizing, public policy model and the nature of human services are discussed.

1.   History of government intervention in human services

The concept of human service as a right for citizens is rooted in the idea of welfare states, and nations are held responsible for the "cradle to grave." To understand this concept, it is important to grasp how governments have become responsible for people's minimum standard of living. This section reviews the history of the concept.

Since early times, social welfare provision has been connected with religion for Jews, Christians, Muslims, Buddhists, and other religions that emphasize the concept of mutual aid. Such religions preach the importance of relief for the socially vulnerable. In fact, many charity organizations today track their histories to religious groups. Zakat, a concept of tithing and alms, is one of the five pillars of Islam. *Shikanin*, built in 593 A.D. by Prince Shotoku,[2] is the oldest surviving social welfare institution in Japan and has a strong Shinto/ Buddhist influence. In European societies, Christian churches functioned as the providers of welfare, and in such ways religion played a significant role in social welfare provision widely across the world during the Middle Ages.

However, following the Protestant Reformation in the 16th century, states little by little began to intervene in the field of social welfare in Europe. Martin Luther (Luther, 1520: 71) stated that beggary was to be eliminated, emphasizing the importance of labor, and John Calvin (Calvin, 1536) criticized the existing arbitrary social welfare, quoting the Biblical phrase: "If man will not work, he shall not eat."[3] As Protestantism became more influential in many European countries, such thinkers gradually changed people's views of the socially vulnerable. As a result, states began to intervene in social welfare to save the economically vulnerable. The Elizabethan Poor Law of 1601 in the United Kingdom was the first legislation on social welfare. In addition, the concept of welfare was added to the French Constitution of 1791.[4] These laws had an influence outside Europe, too; for example, Japan adopted the 1874 social welfare principle *Kekkyu-kisoku*[5] (Kasuno, 1997).

Government intervention in social welfare developed as the governing systems of industrialized nations became democratic in the 19th and 20th centuries. As seen in Table 1.1, the political systems gradually democratized in many countries

Table 1.1 Introduction of universal suffrage, selected countries (year)

Country	Male	Female
France	1848	1944
United States	1870	1920
Germany	1871	1919
United Kingdom	1918	1928
Japan	1925	1945

and, as this occurred, the voice of the socially vulnerable began to influence policies. Shortly after male suffrage was introduced in 1883, for example, the German government decided to provide health insurance for workers; compulsory accident insurance and retirement pensions were introduced in subsequent legislation. These laws signal when government intervention in the social welfare of ordinary citizens—not just the poor—commenced.

Government social welfare provision was further developed in reaction to two historic events in the first half of the 20th century. First, the Great Depression led to the welfare state[6] in many countries. In the United States, as a part of the New Deal program, the Social Security Act of 1935 provided for federally funded financial assistance to the elderly, the blind, and dependent children. In Japan, the National Health Insurance Law, which was especially for those who suffered during the Depression, was enacted in 1938. By the 1930s, most of the world's industrial nations had health insurance and retirement pensions. These trends represented the middle way between communism and capitalism. Moreover, in 1942, the idea of comprehensive cradle-to-grave social welfare services was suggested in the Beveridge report in the United Kingdom.

Second, in the period following World War II, cradle-to-grave welfare programs were implemented in many countries to recover from the damage of the war. In the United Kingdom, the National Insurance Act, the National Assistance Act, and the National Health Service Act came into force in 1948. In Japan, the Child Care Law (*Jido-fukushi hou*) of 1947 and the Mentally/Physically Challenging Care Law (*Shintaishougaisha fukushi hou*) were enacted.

However, not all governments have equally extensive social welfare systems. Esping-Andersen (1990) laid out three main types of welfare state, depending on the degree of government intervention, namely, the liberal, conservative, and social democratic, which are typically represented by the United States, Germany, and Sweden, respectively. Meanwhile, the role of non-governmental organizations continued to be an important provider of social welfare, and they continue to play a significant role in the provision of social welfare in many countries.

Nevertheless, most modern governments are expected to be responsible for ensuring their citizens have a certain standard of living. The OECD was formed in 1960 with the objective of "achieving the highest sustainable economic growth and employment and a rising standard of living in Member countries." In addition, the foundations of welfare-related international organizations, such as the World Health Organization and the United Nations Children's Fund, globally advocated the idea of welfare states. Together with other social welfare services, these organizations contributed to how the provision of human services became a part of governments' responsibility.

Human services began to be provided through the markets alongside an increase in demand for human services during this period, but government interventions in the provision of human services have continued. Davidson (2009: 46–47) cited several reasons for governments' continued interventions in the human service market. First, since the aim of human services is to meet the basic developmental and care needs of people, a strong moral and public nature (commonality) is required to ensure a minimum level of service quality for everyone and to avoid poor services to anyone. Second, it is necessary to customize human services according to the user, and service providers have a great deal of discretion on this point. It is difficult to standardize services, which means it is also difficult to measure effects. Third, there is information asymmetry between the service provider and user in the human service market. Unlike such goods as daily necessities, long-term care is difficult to evaluate via external evaluations of the content and quality of services, and is especially difficult for the general public to understand. Finally, many end users of human services have limited funds to purchase the necessary services.

2. Generalization of the provision of human services through competitive markets

This section explains the factors that have created the care quality problem that is the focus of this book. With specific reference to the case of long-term care, government efforts to maintain the quality of care in a system of market provision, and the problems that continue to hamper these efforts, are described.

OECD countries currently spend large amounts of money on providing long-term care. Table 1.2 illustrates public and private expenditure on long-term care as a percentage of gross domestic product (GDP), although the data are a little old. Total expenditure ranges from below 0.2 percent of GDP in Mexico to almost 3 percent of GDP in Sweden. Most countries, however, range between 0.5 percent and 1.6 percent of GDP; only Norway and Sweden have expenditure ratios well above this level.

In most OECD countries, major portions of the expenditure on long-term care come from public funding. As illustrated in Figure 1.1, in all countries except Spain, public funding is higher than private funding.

Internationally, total spending on long-term care correlates with the share of the very elderly people in the population (80 years and older). Using expenditure figures from the OECD, Figure 1.2 plots the expenditure for long-term care as a percentage of GDP and the percentages of people aged 80 years and older.

Interestingly, the correlation between expenditure and population aged 65 years and older is rather weak, as shown in Figure 1.3. According to the OECD (2005: 20), among the elderly, those who actually need long-term care are generally aged 80 years and older.

The expenditure on long-term care is expected to increase, because the share of elderly people over the age of 80 years in the population is set to further expand. Figure 1.4 shows the percentage of people over the age of 80 years in the populations of all OECD countries for the period 2010 to 2040. Clearly, Japan faces the largest and most immediate challenge with the proportion of people aged over 80 years growing at an accelerated rate from 6.3 to 14 percent each year from 2010 to 2040. In Australia, the rise is from 3.9 percent in 2000 to 7.8 percent in 2010. In the United States, the growth ranges from 3.8 to 7 percent in the same period. In summary, the speed of increase varies from country to country; however, the OECD average percentage is projected to rise to 7.7 percent by 2040 (OECD, 2005).

Table 1.2 Public and private expenditure on long-term care as a percentage of GDP

	Total expenditure			Public expenditure			Private expenditure		
	Home care	*Institutions*	*Total*	*Home care*	*Institutions*	*Total*	*Home care*	*Institutions*	*Total*
Australia	0.38	0.81	1.19	0.30	0.56	0.86	0.08	0.25	0.33
Austria	n.a.	n.a.	n.a.	n.a.	n.a.	1.32	n.a.	n.a.	n.a.
Canada	0.17	1.06	1.23	0.17	0.82	0.99	n.a.	0.24	0.24
Germany	0.47	0.88	1.35	0.43	0.52	0.95	0.04	0.36	0.40
Hungary	< 0.10	< 0.20	< 0.30	n.a.	n.a.	< 0.20	n.a.	n.a.	< 0.10
Ireland	0.19	0.43	0.62	0.19	0.33	0.52	n.a.	0.10	0.10
Japan	0.25	0.58	0.83	0.25	0.51	0.76	0.00	0.07	0.07
Korea	n.a.	n.a.	< 0.30	< 0.10	< 0.10	< 0.20	n.a.	n.a.	n.a.
Luxemburg	n.a.	n.a.	n.a.	0.15	0.37	0.52	n.a.	n.a.	n.a.
Mexico	n.a.	n.a.	< 0.20	n.a.	n.a.	< 0.10	n.a.	n.a.	< 0.10
Netherlands	0.60	0.83	1.44	0.56	0.75	1.31	0.05	0.08	0.13
New Zealand	0.12	0.56	0.68	0.11	0.34	0.45	0.01	0.22	0.23
Norway	0.69	1.45	2.15	0.66	1.19	1.85	0.03	0.26	0.29
Poland	0.35	0.03	0.38	0.35	0.03	0.37	n.a.	0.00	0.00
Spain	0.23	0.37	0.61	0.05	0.11	0.16	0.18	0.26	0.44
Sweden	0.82	2.07	2.89	0.78	1.96	2.74	0.04	0.10	0.14
Switzerland	0.20	1.34	1.54	n.a.	n.a.	n.a.	n.a.	n.a.	n.a.
United Kingdom	0.41	0.96	1.29	0.17	0.58	0.74	0.16	0.39	0.54
United States	0.33	0.96	1.29	0.17	0.58	0.74	0.16	0.39	0.54
Average*	0.38	0.88	1.25	0.35	0.64	0.99	0.06	0.19	0.24

Source: OECD (2005: 26)

Note: Data for Hungary, Korea, Mexico, and Poland are only rough indicators of magnitude. Data for Australia, Norway, Spain, and Sweden are for the age group 65+ years. "n.a." indicates not available. To be comparative, all data are as of the year 2000.

*Average excludes Austria, Hungary, Luxemburg, Korea, and Mexico

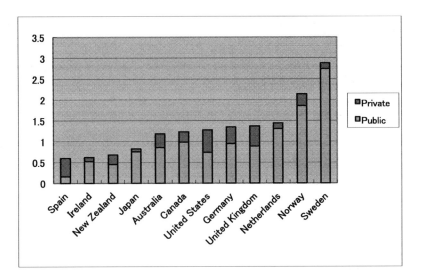

Figure 1.1 Public and private expenditure on long-term care as a percentage of GDP
Source: See Table 1.2

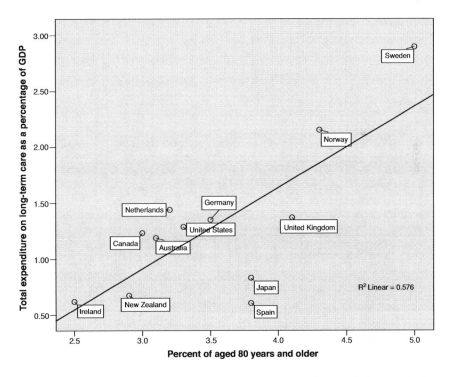

Figure 1.2 Correlation between total long-term care spending and the population share of very old people (Aged 80+)[7]

Source: Table 1.2 and United Nations (2012)

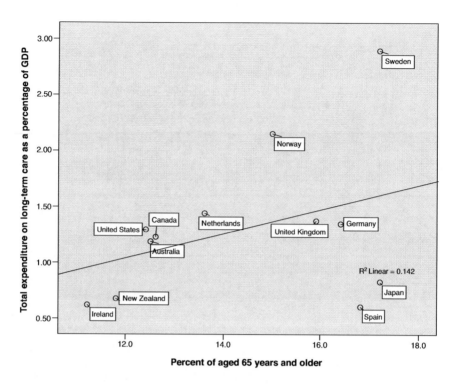

Figure 1.3 Correlation between total long-term care spending and population share of older people (aged 65+)

Source: Table 2.1 and United Nations (2008)

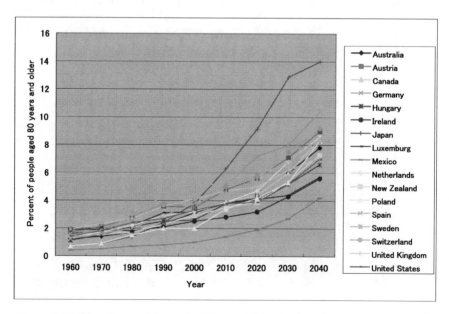

Figure 1.4 Share of very old people (80+ years) in the population, 1960 to 2040

Source: United Nations (2008)

Note: Data for Korea are not available.

The problem of providing long-term care for a growing percentage of the population is compounded by the existence of fewer taxpayers. In most OECD countries, the ratio of people aged 65 years and older to the population aged 20–64 years is growing. As Table 1.3 shows, the old age-dependency ratio will continue to expand. This means there will be (a) fewer people to support the older population and (b) possible limitations on the budget for long-term care

Table 1.3 Old age-dependency ratio (1960–2040)

Ratio of people 65+ years to the population 20–64 years

	1960	*2000*	*2040*	*Change in % points*	
				1960–2000	*2000–2040*
Australia	15.8	20.7	43.8	4.9	23
Austria	21.1	25.1	59	4	33.9
Belgium	20.4	28.2	51.2	7.7	23
Canada	14.7	20.3	43.6	5.6	23.2
Czech Republic	15.2	21.9	47.8	6.8	25.9
Denmark	19	24.1	44.4	5.2	20.3
Finland	13.4	24.6	49.8	11.2	25.1
France	20.8	27.5	50	6.7	22.5
Germany	–	26.4	54.5	–	28.1
Greece	14.0	28.3	57.9	14.3	29.6
Hungary	15.5	24.5	38.4	8.9	13.9
Iceland	16.1	20.4	41	4.3	20.6
Ireland	22.4	19.2	37.7	–3.2	18.5
Italy	15.9	29.1	63.9	13.2	34.8
Japan	10.6	27.9	59.9	17.4	31.9
Korea	6.4	11.4	43.5	4.9	32.1
Luxemburg	17.6	23	36.9	5.4	13.9
Mexico	11.3	9	26	–2.4	17.1
Netherlands	16.9	21.9	48.1	5	26.1
New Zealand	17	20.1	48.2	3.1	28.1
Norway	19.8	25.7	42.9	6	17.2
Poland	11.1	20.3	41.1	9.2	20.8
Portugal	14.5	26.7	46.3	12.2	19.6
Slovak Republic	12.8	18.8	39.4	6	20.6
Spain	14.5	27.2	55.7	12.7	28.5
Sweden	20.2	29.5	46.7	9.3	17.2
Switzerland	17.6	24.9	63.9	7.3	39
Turkey	7.5	10.7	23.9	3.1	13.2
United Kingdom	20.1	26.9	46.3	6.8	19.4
United States	17.6	21.1	37.9	3.4	16.8
OECD average	15.9	22.9	46.3	6.9	23.5

Source: OECD (2005)

Note: Germany 1960 (before reunification) was not comparable with 2000 data.

due to the decreasing share of the working (tax-paying) population. Governments will need to become more efficient at providing long-term care.

There are, however, positive ways of looking at these demographic arguments.
Knichman and Snell (2002) argue that reductions in the number of children
with care is needed to offset some of the increase in older people needing care.
Moreover, not many people in the 65–74 age group actually require long-term
care and an increasing share of people in that age group contribute to providing
care and supervision to both young people and the very old. This improves the
ratio of potential caregivers to those needing care, as part of the elderly genera-
tion are transferred to those requiring "long-term care."

Nevertheless, the utility of these positive views might be rendered redundant
by prolonged life expectancies. Demographic forecasts are problematic, because
the factors driving mortality decline, particularly at a higher age, and are poorly
understood (OECD, 2005: 100). In the past, demographers and actuaries
consistently underestimated predictions of life expectancy (Cutler and Maera,
2001; Wilmoth, 1998). Therefore, it is possible that the dependency ratio of
very old people will be even greater than expected.

Changes in people's lifestyles might be another factor that increases demand
for long-term care. These changes include decreasing family size, greater life
expectancy for older people, geographical dispersion of families, and the tendency
for women to be educated and to work outside the home in most countries
(Figure 1.5). Thus, the young can no longer afford to play the role of caregiver
for their elderly family members.

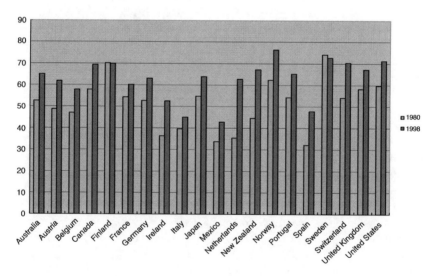

Figure 1.5 Female labor force participation rate

Source: *Labour Force Statistics,* OECD (2000)

Female labor force of all ages divided by female population of 15–64 years

Note: The following data were not available: Czech Republic, Denmark, Hungary, Iceland,
Korea, Poland, and Turkey. The data for Germany in 1980 are for former West Germany.

What is certain is that the demand for long-term care will continue to increase in OECD member nations. Governments will have to respond to these increasing needs with increasingly limited resources.

Market provision of long-term care began around the mid-1960s. The United States initiated market utilization, in general, in 1980. Since then, other governments, including the United Kingdom, Germany, and Japan, have gradually implemented marketization. Long-term care services provided by the market are likely to increase in the future. Table 1.4 lists the benchmark events in the market provision of long-term care in selected countries.

In the United States, the utilization of the market was greatly encouraged under the Reagan administration. Regulations related to home and community long-term care were reduced and eligibilities for Medicare and Medicaid were expanded. Since then, the market for nursing homes has increased 9.5 percent on average from 1986 to 1995 and the market for home care grew 19.6 percent in the same period (MHLW, 2000).

In the United Kingdom, local municipalities traditionally provided elderly care, but there have been major changes since 1992 with Community Care Reform. This changed the system from the direct provision of services by local governments to the purchase of services from the non-government sector (private

Table 1.4 Benchmark events in the history of long-term care policies in selected countries (1965–2000)

Year	Country	Event
1965	US	Enactment of Medicare and Medicaid.
		Medicaid (medical support for low-income citizens) began to support nursing home fees, including private nursing homes.
1966	Australia	The federal government commenced grants for nursing homes, including private ones.
1969	US	The Department of Housing and Urban Development began supporting the opening of new nursing homes, including private ones.
1980	US	Amendment of the Social Security Act.
		Medicaid covered the fees for home care (assisted living) services, including private organizations.
1980	UK	The Supplementary Benefit Regulations of 1980 supported private nursing homes.
1981	US	Enactment of the Home and Community-based Long-term Waver Option authorized state use of Medicare.
1985	Australia	The Aged Care Reform Strategy started.
		The Home and Community Care Act encouraged assisted living services.

(Continued)

Table 1.4 (Continued)

Year	Country	Event
1989	Germany	Enactment of health reform, which enabled assisted living services to include medical activities.
1989	Japan	The government began to utilize private companies by outsourcing nursing home services.
1990	UK	Enactment of the National Health Service and Community Care Act.
1990	US	Personal care benefits authorized states to allow personal care attendants to accompany clients and provide services outside the home.
1990	Japan	Amendment of Social Welfare Laws. Decentralization of government involvement in social welfare encouraged private companies to provide long-term care services.
1991	Australia	The federal government lifted the ban on the private sector's participation in hostels.[8]
1991	Australia	Financial support for those who were eligible to stay at hostels commenced.
1992	UK	The Community Care Act was implemented, encouraging the utilization of the private sector in long-term care provision.
1992	Sweden	Edel Reform (1998). The transformation of the authority of long-term medical facilities from *landstings* to *kommuns* encouraged the private sector to enter the elderly care market.
1993	UK	Community Care Reform.
1994	Germany	Establishment of Long-Term Care Insurance.
1995	Germany	The private sector entered service provision for assisted living care (home care).
1996	UK	The Community Care (Direct Payment) Act of 1996 encouraged assisted living care.
1995	Germany	Introduction of Long-Term Care Insurance (*Pflege-Versicherung*).
1997	France	Establishment of the Law of Long-term Care.
2000	Japan	Introduction of Long-Term Care Insurance (*Kaigo hoken*).

companies and non-profits). After this major shift, care managers from local authorities had to estimate the demands of those who needed care and prepare a comprehensive care plan. This resulted in the expansion of non-government elderly care provision (MHLW, 2000).

Traditionally, in Germany, elderly care services were mainly provided by six philanthropic organizations, including the Red Cross and Caritas. The government gave them financial support and the market share of these six organizations exceeded 50 percent of the entire sector of long-term care services. However, with the introduction of Long-Term Care Insurance (LTCI) in 1995, the government began giving financial support to non-profit organizations and private companies outside of the six philanthropic organizations. Since then, many companies and non-profit organizations have entered the market (MHLW, 2000).

In Australia, private philanthropies that received financial support from the government traditionally provided nursing home services. Then, in order to respond to diversified public needs, the government implemented the Aged Care Reform Strategy in 1985. As a result, financial support for hostel services for lower dependency elderly began in 1991. Moreover, based on the Home and Community Care Act, assisted living services have been increasingly provided by the non-government sector with support from the government (Australian Institute of Health and Welfare, 1995).

In Sweden, which is known as a social democracy, elderly care is mainly provided by the public sector. However, utilization of the non-government sector has gradually increased since the Edel Reform of 1992. This tendency can be seen, especially in big cities, such as Stockholm and Gothenburg, where assisted living services are in demand (MHLW, 2000).

Finally, in Japan, since the enactment of the Long-Term Care for Older People Law (*Rojin fukushi hou*) of 1963, public institutions have predominantly provided long-term care services. However, since the late 1980s, long-term care services from the private sector have gradually increased. The Long-Term Care Insurance Law of 2000 deregulated private sector access to the market for almost all elderly services and currently, about 40 percent of long-term care providers are private companies (MHLW, 2002).

These changes mean that to a certain extent, the market currently plays a significant role in the provision of long-term care in most OECD countries. The study lacks accurate data to compare the forms of long-term care service provision internationally owing to the absence of a tangible measurement of providers' share.[9] Nevertheless, from the estimates of Nissei Life Insurance Research Institute (1998) (see Table 1.5), we can observe that currently, the market plays a major role and is the main provider of these services in both the

Table 1.5 Long-term care provision by the private sector in selected countries

Institution by the private sector		*Home care by the private sector*	
United States	75%	Japan	70%
United Kingdom	60%	The United States	65%
Germany	45%	Germany	50%
Japan	40%	Sweden	8%
Australia	30%		

Source: Nissei Life Insurance Research Institute (1998)

Note: The rest of the above indications are provided by both governments and non-profit organizations.

United States and United Kingdom, although the data are a little old. In Japan, Germany, and Australia, about half of the provision of these long-term care services relies on the private sector.

3. Quality problem in the long-term care market

A significant challenge of marketization is how to ensure care quality. Like any other field of human service, long-term care covers a very diverse field of needs. Although much research has been undertaken on this issue to ensure service quality in markets, there is still some room for improvement.

Governments have tried hard to deal with this through care quality assurance. Table 1.6 lists care quality assurance policies on long-term care in the United States, United Kingdom, Germany, Australia, and Japan. Service providers that do not follow these policies are punished, and depending on the situation, eliminated from the market. A user's choice should, therefore, eliminate the provision of poor quality care and eventually meet the user's needs.

Surprisingly, however, these efforts have not been producing results. The public's dissatisfaction with the quality of care has not been addressed and can be said to have reached serious levels. The OECD (2005) claimed that the poor quality of long-term care provision was still a common issue. Even the United Kingdom, which has the longest history of implementation of long-term care provision using license subsidies (LS), has not been able to solve this problem. In fact, Harrington (2001) reported that despite efforts towards quality control, poor quality care for the 1.6 million people in nursing homes has existed for

Table 1.6 Care quality assurance policies for long-term care provision in OECD countries

Country	System
US	Home Care Quality Assurance Act of 1987
	Omnibus Budget Reconciliation Act of 1987
	State-level long-term care service guidelines
UK	Registered Homes Act (1984)
Germany	Quality Form system (voluntary)
Australia	Aged or Disabled Persons Act of 1972
	Nursing Home Assistance Act of 1974
	Home and Community Care Act of 1986: investigations of the Standard Monitoring Team
	Aged Care Act of 1997: introduction of Accreditation Standards (1998)
Sweden	Customer questionnaire survey by communities
	Facility inspection by the Handicap Institute
Japan	Introduction of yearly inspections by local municipalities, as well as third-party evaluators (2001)

25 years in the United States. There are worldwide accounts in the media of the abuse and neglect of frail, elderly people, both in nursing homes and in community care (Braithwaite, 2001: 443). Although governments have implemented quality assurance policies, the problem of unsatisfactory care provision has not been completely solved.

4. Public policy model

The previous sections identify longstanding care quality issues in the market with the following chronological steps.

1   Due to the notion of welfare states, governments need to ensure the provision of human services.
2   Due to financial and technical constraints, governments need to provide the necessary human services through a competitive market instead of through direct provision.
3   In order to assure the quality of care in a competitive market, which tends to sacrifice service quality for profit maximization, governments have implemented various regulatory policies.
4   However, unsatisfactory care quality issues remain in the market.

The findings indicate that the established enabling/outsourcing policies regarding the human service market are not effective.

The next step is to examine possible causes of the problem. To do so, we need to step back from the field of human services and investigate the care quality problem in the bigger picture of the public policy model. It can be assumed that the current market-utilizing public policy model has defects, because the care quality problems of human service provision remain, in spite of governments' efforts. Certainly, the market-utilizing public policy model behind outsourced public service provision has improved the quality of services in many fields such as telecommunication services, parcel delivery services, and public transportation. Nonetheless, the model has not been able to apply as effectively to human service provision. The next section reviews the public policy model and investigates the causes of the long-term care quality issues in human service provision.

4.1. *From bureaucracy to market utilization*

The public policy model has gradually shifted from bureaucracy to market utilization. This section first gives an overview of the transition. Then it investigates the different outcomes between human services and other public services.

The history of the public policy model begins in the late 19th century. One of the earliest contributions to the field of public administration was made by Max Weber, the German sociologist and economist, who believed that the requirements of the Industrial Age necessitated the use of a highly centralized, rule-bound, expert-driven hierarchic system in public sector management. This form of organization represents a bureaucracy.

For the first half of the 20th century, bureaucracy was assumed the best method for providing public services (Ostrom, 1989). According to Albrow (1970), the elements of bureaucracy include developing a division of labor and specialization of function, establishing a hierarchy with clearly defined roles and explicit rules, and making employment decisions (e.g., selection and promotion) based on merit.

The idea of bureaucracy was widely accepted because it fit very well with the social needs at the time. Bureaucracy was originally developed to accommodate the needs of mass production in the Industrial Age. Furthermore, bureaucracy was required in response to far-reaching events, such as the Great Depression and the First and Second World Wars. Because of the success of bureaucracy, public administration, as a model of organization, became associated with a belief in social engineering to correct market failure (Boyne, 1996).

However, bureaucracy began to expose its functional fragilities once the post-war period was over. The biggest factor was the growing diversity of the needs for public service. The industrial structure had gradually shifted from heavy knowledge (e.g., iron and steel) to compact (e.g., service) knowledge. Human service was required to respond to detailed care needs. In response to this trend, bureaucracy was a rigid administrative model (Dubois, 1979). Certainly, bureaucratic forms of organization are stable conditions, but they have difficulty learning from their mistakes and are slow in adapting to changing circumstances (Burns and Stalker, 1961; Crozier, 1964). In fact, the features of bureaucracy began to be criticized as weaknesses. For example, Dunleavy and O'Leary (1987) claimed that the assumption of a clear distinction between policies/policymaking and administration had been found to be impractical. Merton (1952) argued that the rule-governed basis of bureaucracy was dysfunctional because the means tended to displace the ends, resulting in the punctilious adherence to rules.

Furthermore, the assumption of bureaucracy that politicians and administration staff act in the public interest began to be criticized as naïve. Many researchers, such as Crozier (1964); Selznick (1949); and Tullock (1970), argued that public employees do not have a special type of motivation, but act in order to maximize their self-interest in terms of income, prestige, and power. The authors claimed that this resulted in state budget inflation, that public officials increased their authority by maximizing their department budgets, and that politicians worked for their ambitions by spending a lot of public money to secure their votes.

As a result, the idea of public choice became more accepted as a solution to these problems. It appeared to be a way of addressing the human behavior of self-interest by minimizing the role of the state, limiting the discretionary power of politicians, reducing public monopolies to a minimum, and maximizing the use of the market. That is, proponents of public choice seemed to recognize that, as departments have vested self-interest, they should not both advise on policy and implement it; the public choice solution claimed that advisory, regulatory, and delivery functions should be separated and undertaken by different agencies (Boston, 1991).

Many academics reinforce the challenges of public service provision through markets. In fact, the phenomenon goes by several names: government by proxy (Kettl, 1993), third-party government (Salamon, 1989; Smith and Lipsky, 1993), hollow government, the hollow state (Milward, 1994, 1996), virtual government (Sturgess, 1996), the hollow crown (Weller *et al.*, 1997), shadow government, and the contracting regime (Kettl, 1988). The argument is that public organization needs management, not administration, where public management means the fulfillment of goals rather than the careful observation of procedures (Lane, 1993).

Ideas to introduce managerial methods into the public sector developed apace during the 1970s and 1980s. This trend emphasized focusing on the ends, not the means, as well as the establishment of semi-autonomous public sector agencies in which managers were given greater discretion to manage. By the 1990s, this distinctive approach to public sector management, new public management (NPM), was shaped by both private sector management techniques and ideas from public choice theory. This trend emerged in many OECD countries (Hood, 1991; Hughes, 1998). The ideas of NPM, according to Aulich *et al.* (2001), are summarized in Table 1.7.

The overall transition of public administration theories toward market utilization is identified in Table 1.8. The two public administration theories listed in Table 1.8 describe the transition from centralized bureaucratic models to networked/outsourced market-oriented models in terms of the provision of public

Table 1.7 The ideas of new public management

- A shift from input controls and rules to a reliance on quantifiable output measures and performance targets
- Separation of policymaking from service delivery
- Disaggregation of large bureaucratic structures into quasi-autonomous and specific purpose agencies
- Contractual relationship between decentralized service providers and central service purchasers
- Preference for private ownership, outsourcing, and contestability in public service provision
- The pursuit of the user for greater efficiency of public funds by
  - greater publication of performance information,
  - targets for efficiency savings,
  - the introduction of competition where possible, and
  - strengthened audit arrangements.
- More commercial styles of management practice, including
  - human resource management policies (e.g., short-term labor contracts and performance-related reward systems),
  - strategic and business planning,
  - internal trading arrangements,
  - flatten organizational hierarchies,
  - greater customer orientation, and
  - revised corporate governance arrangements.

Table 1.8 Transformation of Public Administration Model

Characterization	Traditional public bureaucracy	Market utilization
Dominant values	Administration	Competition
Performance measure	Process	Outcome
Role of government	Dominant provider	Enabler/purchaser
Structure	Centralized and hierarchical	Networked, outsourced
State fiscal policy	Broad	Narrow, contracted spending
Relative importance of public and private sectors	Public sector dominant	Private sector dominant

Source: Aulich *et al.* (2001)

services. The left-hand side was designed to capture the traditional model of public administration, dominated by process, inputs, hierarchy, and the use of the public sector for service delivery. In the right-hand side, the role of the market (i.e., private sector) expanded and that of the public sector contracted in the provision of services, and competition and outcomes became crucial in public service provision. Within each model, there is room for substantial variation in practice. In some countries, it is possible to recognize a sequence of stages in public sector reform, with movement flowing from the traditional administrative state to the market state.

5.   Causes of long-term care quality issues in human service provision

Up to this point, we have seen that public service provision today is through market utilization. However, the features of market utilization have caused the long-standing care quality issues practically only in human service provision. These features have fundamentally clashed with the earlier mentioned nature of human services in two ways.

"Competition" is a dominant value of the market-utilizing public policy model and this conflicts with the requirement for discretion in human service provision. As the needs of human service are quite diverse,[10] providers need to customize their services for each individual user. However, this indicates that users need to carefully observe quality, as well as price, when purchasing a service. The quality of care services inevitably varies by provider. The purchasing market model is expressed as $Y = x\ (p,\ q)$, where p is price and q is quality; the model accommodates both inexpensive but of poor quality, and expensive but of good quality. Consider the following example: some long-term care providers respectfully respond to every single need of care recipients while other providers neglect care recipients and sometimes even abuse them physically and mentally. This model is simply not acceptable in public service provision, because, unlike that of consumer items, any poor quality treatment in public services often causes significant damage to the lives of people who rely on them for every aspect of their lives.

This conflict is unique in human services. In most other public services, which do not customize the services provided, all users receive a similar level of quality. This means that the market model works as $\Upsilon = xp$. In successful cases, such as telecommunication services, delivery services, and public transportation, the players in the market treat all users equally.[11] As a result, the quality of these services is standardized. For instance, Japan Railways (JR) runs trains just like other private railway companies do in Japan, and there are no differences between them in terms of safety and punctuality. It is the same overseas. Internet connection services provided by Telstra are very similar to those by Optus in Australia, and the speed of both internet connections is at the same level. In the United States, the United States Postal Service (USPS), United Parcel Service of America (UPS), and FedEx deliver parcels in a similar way and their punctuality is at more or less the same level. Such similarities have led to the success of this provision through the market. Due to simple price competition in the market, (i.e., $\Upsilon = xp$), the players become financially motivated to enhance the efficiency of the service provision. Therefore, the productivity of the supply is improved and the expenses of governments and consumers are minimized.

Competition alone, however, does not translate into similar success in the human service sector. Discretion in the provision of human services inevitably produces diverse levels of service quality. The existing public policy model cannot be applied unchanged, and within competition, mechanisms must be devised to ensure service quality. Nonetheless, the existing model does not do so. By including quality q together with price p in the equation of the market equilibrium model, the market-utilizing public policy model accommodates a range of service quality from extremely good to completely unacceptable, in terms of human welfare and dignity. This is a long-term service quality issue.

For governments to solve the care quality issue, first they must overcome the contradiction between competition and providers' discretion. Since such discretion is necessary for human service provision, governments need to redesign the market to control competition.

> *How should governments design the human service market in order to ensure service quality?*

This question is answered in Part I of this book.

Another important question that remains is how to measure the quality of care. What is good quality of care and how can we measure it? Conflict occurs in performance measurement; that is, a fundamental disagreement exists between the outcomes-oriented public policy model and the ambiguous policy goals of human service.

Measuring outcomes inevitably requires tangible goals. Since a policy's outcomes indicate how much the policy has achieved its goals, the goals need to be clear; otherwise, it is not possible to measure them.

Nonetheless, the policy goals of human service tend to be ambiguous (Lipsky, 1980). Statements like "long-term care for the peaceful and respected life of elderly people" are not measurable. How can one objectively measure the peacefulness of, or the respect for, someone's life? Some people might consider the user's satisfaction a useful measure, but we must not forget that a significant number of long-term care users suffer from dementia.

Indeed, such ambiguity is unique to human service markets. The performances of many other public services provided through the market are measurable. For instance, the safety and accuracy of public transportation are measurable by the accident rate and delay time, respectively. This is also the case with telecommunication and delivery services.

Since the outcomes of human service are not measurable, governments need to introduce an alternative approach. This leads to the second research question of this book.

How should governments set performance measurement?

Part II of this book investigates this problem.

Notes

1 See, for example, Gomez-Ibanez and Meyer (1993) and Li and Xu (2004).
2 There is disagreement about the year of construction.
3 Taken from the New Testament, "St. Paul's Second Letter to the Thessalonians."
4 The constitution mentioned public intervention in social welfare.
5 This principle was to educate the people. The government did not owe any responsibility, but it was the first time for the government to step into social welfare issues in modern Japan.
6 The term "welfare state" was coined by the Allies as a contrast to the "warfare state" of the Axis powers (Megginson and Netter, 2001).
7 The term "very old people" used in the OECD (2005) indicates those aged 80 years or above.
8 In Austria, a hostel is a type of nursing home for lower dependency residents whereas a home for higher dependency residents is called a nursing home.
9 For example, there is a lack of data on the number of institutions, capacity, or income base.
10 For instance, the needs of long-term care vary with the individual.
11 That is, train services treat all passengers equally, compared with human service providers who cannot treat care recipients who are at different levels of care needs in the same way.

Part I

Care market model for the human service market

2 The care market model

The purpose of Part I is to establish how the human service market should be designed in order to maintain capacity and ensure service quality. To do so, this chapter first identifies problems with the existing market model, and then presents an alternative, the CMM, to establish how the human service market should be designed. Thereafter, Chapters 3–5 justify the CMM in terms of its applicability, efficacy, and financial sustainability, respectively.

1. What is the care market model?

In this book, the term "market model" indicates a market design that directs market competition in terms of care quality. In competitive markets, providers naturally aim for profit maximization and behave opportunistically. As a result, they provide services within a wide range of quality and purchasers who do not have money are discriminated against or ignored. This is not a bad characteristic in the consumer products market. However, it is a serious problem in the field of human services, which are provided to ensure people maintain a minimum standard of living. Moreover, expectations about the standard quality of human service care have arisen over time. In long-term care, for example, ADL support is used to cover limited areas, such as meal preparation and room cleaning, but has now been extended to include mental aspects, such as reduction of isolation and depression. Thus, a market model must automatically improve the level of care quality in the market, not only eliminate low-quality service and opportunistic behavior, as if it does not automatically improve the level of care quality in the market, it will not satisfy the minimum expected level.

The current market model is derived from earlier research by Scanlon (1980), which modeled access to nursing homes. At the time of the research, many nations applied a means-tested policy (e.g., Medicaid in the United States) and mainly used private companies to provide long-term care. Using this as a basis, Scanlon (1980) assumed that nursing homes maximized profits π from two types of care recipients: private and Medicaid. In this model, private care recipients pay p and have demand $x(p)$. The nursing home receives reimbursement rate r for each Medicaid care recipient. The total bed supply is $\bar{x}$. Costs $c(\bar{x})$

are the same for private and Medicaid care recipients. Therefore, as long as the nursing home is full, total costs are fixed. Nursing homes maximize profits with respect to private price.

$$\max_{p} \pi = px(p) + r(\bar{x} - x(p)) - c(\bar{x}).$$

(1)

As the quality of care became an issue in long-term care provision, many authors expanded Scanlon's model to quality of care (Dusansky, 1989; Gertler, 1989, 1992; Gertler and Waldman, 1992; Nyman, 1985). Norton (2000) compiled those models into one model, assuming that private care recipients care about quality and that the cost function depends on quality. The model is described in the following formula (2).

$$\max_{p,q} \pi = px(p,q) + r(\bar{x} - x(p,q)) - c(q|\bar{x}).$$

(2)

The nursing home takes Medicaid reimbursement r and its own bed supply $\bar{x}$ as given, and chooses private price p and quality of care q to maximize profits π.

This model does not possess the mechanism to enhance the quality of care in order to solve the problem of poor quality of care. As argued in Chapter 1, the market model that possesses both price and quality components, at the same time, will inevitably accommodate inexpensive but poor quality service as well as expensive but good quality service. The following section further explains the weaknesses of the model.

2.   Problems with the existing market model

The existing market model cannot direct market competition to enhance the quality of care. First, Medicaid care recipients might not pay attention to care quality, since reimbursement rate r is independent of care needs and care quality.[1] In other words, Medicaid care recipients go to nursing homes not necessarily because they really need care (the Medicare reimbursement is in-kind[2] only), and if recipients do not actually need care, they probably are not concerned about the quality of care.[3] The nursing home, on the other hand, responds to recipients' needs opportunistically; nursing homes admit Medicare recipients who require a smaller amount of care in order to minimize their costs. Moreover, nursing homes make more profits by increasing care recipients' reimbursements, despite the quality of care they provide. Therefore, the nursing home tends to provide lower quality of care with an increase in the Medicaid reimbursement rate, because the pool of care recipients able to pay for quality care shrinks (Norton, 2000). This reduction of the private care recipients' ratio raises the marginal cost of quality among the remaining private care recipients and results in reduced quality. Nyman (1988) found that in markets in which excess demand was likely, an increased percentage of Medicaid care recipients were associated with lower quality of care. By contrast, where excess demand was unlikely, an increased percentage of Medicaid care recipients were unrelated to lower quality care. Therefore, in the existing market model, the market does not possess the mechanism to improve quality of care, since a group of users in the market does not care about the quality of care.

Second, although private care recipients pay for a quality, the market model does not eliminate poor quality of care from the market. Figure 2.1 illustrates the behavior of private care recipients in the quality of the market model. As the market model deals with price and quality for care recipients choosing a provider, it can be assumed that care recipients look for high-quality care (q) and inexpensiveness per unit of care (i).[4] The indifference curve (U) represents care recipients in different combinations of high quality and inexpensiveness: $U = u(q, i)$. Note that the price becomes *inexpensive* to the right of the figure, unlike many other charts in microeconomics. That is, at each point on the curve, care recipients do not prefer high quality over inexpensiveness and vice versa. The line ($y = qx + ix$) indicates the necessary care amount for care recipients. Therefore, the utility of care recipients (U) is commonly maximized at (X^*): the breaker point of the indifference curve and the necessary amount of care ($y = qx + ix$). Importantly, nevertheless, the scale of (q) and (i) is unique to each care recipient. The demand for lower quality care continues to exist as long as there are care recipients who do not have the financial resources and are unable to pay privately for expensive and good quality care (e.g., non-wealthy private care recipients). The quality (q^*) is very poor and at a level that cannot be tolerated if the price (i.e., inexpensiveness) (i^*) is very cheap. Therefore, the existing market model does not solve the issue of low care quality.

It might be considered that governments can still eliminate poor quality of care via regulatory policies. In the existing market model, however, the workability of

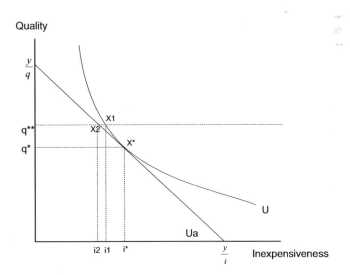

Figure 2.1 Care differentiation and equilibrium

regulations is very limited. Suppose governments intervene in the market and remove quality below (q^{**}), setting (q^{**}) as the minimum quality standard. Care recipients, then, feel that the care level (q^{**}) is too expensive, because (q^{**}) meets the necessary care amount line $(y = qx + ix)$ at $(X2)$, which is located on the left (i.e., expensive) side from the break point $(X1)$, where care recipients feel happy about the quality–inexpensiveness combination. In other words, care recipients observe that (q^{**}) is overpriced as much as $(i1 - i2)$. As a result, care recipients are dissatisfied with the minimum quality standard and some even lose access to long-term care because of the price rise.

3.   Origin of problems with the existing market model

The origin of the problems with the existing market model is that discussions on the market design have taken place separately in the respective fields. In other words, the discussion about the optimal form that the spread of human services should take, as well as proposals and verification for the market design to provide it, has not taken place in an integrated manner. In each field, sociologists are strongly interested in discussing social integration, economists in economic efficiency, political scientists in conflict between social hierarchies, and social policy researchers on the redistribution of wealth to the poor and emergency measures to improve poverty (Castles *et al.*, 2010; Nishimura, 2014). In this way, there has been a noticeable lack of an integrated discussion that transcends the boundaries of these fields. In fact, *The Oxford Handbook of Welfare States*, which is a comprehensive handbook of welfare policy research published in 2010, created by 5 editors and more than 70 authors, concluded that when conducting research into welfare, sticking to the viewpoint of a certain field is damaging, and strongly highlighted the importance of having wide interest and understanding across the various fields (Castles *et al.*, 2010: 149). Nishimura (2014), while referring to this book, also pointed to its importance (Nishimura, 2014: 44).

If everyone were to observe only one part of the whole picture, even if correctly, there would be times when the discussion did not develop holistically. According to the Indian proverb, "The Blind Men and the Elephant," the blind man who feels the elephant's legs concludes they are like pillars, the blind man who touches its tail states it is like a rope, the blind man who touches the elephant's trunk decides it is like a tree branch, and the blind man who touches its tusk decides it is like a pipe. In this way, none alone obtains an image of the elephant as a whole. In the same way, sociologists and political scientists discuss the form the provision of welfare should take, but do not verify its efficacy, while economists discuss and verify the market's economic efficiency, but do not participate actively in the discussion on the form that the market should take and that is a prerequisite to economic efficiency.

In fact, the discussion on market design has not been deepened since the market model (2) of Norton (2000). This conclusion applies not only to the literature in English, but also the Japanese literature. For example, since the introduction of LTCE in 2000, including the pioneering study of Shimono *et al.* (2003), who systematically summarized the economic analyses of long-term care service, all discussions on the modeling and verification of human services and, specifically, the long-term care market have been premised on the existing market design. Of course, some studies have discussed the type of social security there should be in the market from the perspective of economics, such as Oshio (2005, 2013, 2014); Nishimura (2014); Nishimura *et al.* (2014); and Tachibanaki (2010). However, these studies strongly had introductory implications, as case studies of other countries and as the premises for the discussion, and they did not actually model or verify the optimum sort of market mechanism for the purpose of human services. Thus, today, the debate on the model presented by Norton (2000) has not been developed.

The reason that modeling and verification research has not been conducted is related to the usability of data. This requires an understanding of the conventional data usage environment. First, there are two types of assumptions in the market model in the human service field. The first is that it is a universal care system, that the state has the responsibility to provide care to all citizens regardless whether they are rich or poor. The second is means tested, in which the government has the responsibility to provide care limited to the economically vulnerable only. Theoretically, both systems are mechanisms to prevent people from being separated from the human service market. Actually, around half of OECD members have introduced a universal system, and the other half have introduced a care system limited to the economically vulnerable[5] (Table 2.1).

In fact, up to now, all market models analyzed in the previous research in the long-term care field assumed a system of care limited to the economically vulnerable. A feature of the previous research is that almost all of it on the model can be explained by the fact that it originated from the United States, which adopts a system of care limited to the economically vulnerable. Problems with the quality of care in the long-term care market have been reported on throughout the world and it is a problem shared by many countries, but the disclosure of information on the quality of care by service providers has been limited. In most cases, the information is limited to public institutions, by region, or limited to a specific region. Up until recently, only the United States required the disclosure of information on care quality by all nursing homes, and thus, naturally, researchers have built models by assuming the United States system, which is limited to the economically vulnerable. Conversely, precisely because of this, it can be said that empirical research on the form the market model should take has not been developed since Norton (2000). The existing market model is not suitable for human service purposes and needs to be reconstructed. In this sort of situation, in terms of the subjects of the analysis of the model, the environment is biased toward a care system limited to the economically vulnerable, which has become a factor behind the narrowing of the ideas for the model's reconstruction.

Table 2.1 Major public long-term care program in 19 selected OECD member countries

	Type of care	Program	Type
S. Korea	Home care Institutional care	Long-Term Care Insurance	Universal
Luxemburg	Home care Institutional care	Dependency insurance	Universal
Mexico	Institutional care	Specialized services in geriatrics	All ages, all people who are insured
	Home care	Day centers for pensioners and retired	Insured pensioners and retired people
Netherlands	Home care	AWBZ	All ages Universal
	Institutional care	AWBZ	All ages Universal
New Zealand	Home care	Carer Support	Means-tested
		Home Support: home help	Means-tested
	Institutional care	Long-term residential care	Means-tested
Norway	Home care	Public long-term care	Universal
	Institutional care	Public long-term care	Universal
Poland	Home care Institutional care	Social services	Means-tested
Spain	Home care Institutional care	Social care programs at Autonomous Community level	Means-tested
Sweden	Home care Institutional care	Programs at Canton level; health promotion for the elderly by Old Age Insurance	Universal
Switzerland	Home care Institutional care	Programs at Canton level; health promotion for the elderly by Old Age Insurance	Means-tested for institutional care
United Kingdom		Social service	Means-tested
	Home care (cash)	Social Security Benefits	Means-tested
Australia	Institutional care	Residential care	Partly means-tested
	Home care	Community Aged Care Package (CACP)	Means-tested

	Type of care	Program	Type
		Home and community care (HACC)	Means-tested
		Carer allowance	Means-tested
Austria	Home care	Long-term care allowance	Universal
	Institutional care	Long-term care allowance	Universal
Canada	Home care	Provincial programs	Usually means-tested
	Institutional care	Provincial programs	Usually means-tested
Germany	Home care	Social Long-term Care Insurance	Universal
	Institutional care	Social Long-term Care Insurance	Universal
Hungary	Home care/ Institutional care	Social protection and social care provision program	Means-tested
Ireland	Institutional care	Nursing Home Subvention Scheme	Means-tested
		Public long-term care	Means-tested
	Home care	Community-based care	Partly means-tested
Japan	Home care	Long-term Care	Universal
	Institutional care	Insurance System	
United States	Home care (in-kind)	Medicaid	Means-tested
	Insurance care (in-kind)		

Source: South Korea: Choi (2009); others: OECD (2005)

4. CMM: directing market competition to improve care quality

This book focuses on the rise of Japan as an opposing force for this problem. As a result of reforms of recent years, Japan publishes all information on the quality of care by community-based service providers.[7] Under the LTCI system introduced in 2000, which is based on the universal system, Japan mandated a third-party evaluation system for community-based service providers in 2006 and has been accumulating data on them. The contribution of this book is that it presents a new care market model (CMM) as an alternative to the existing market model that encapsulates the problem of low-quality long-term care by understanding this change to the environment for using data on Japan's long-term care market, which assumes universal care.

Next, the existing market model is modified in two ways. The first modification is to remove the care recipients who do not care about quality of care from the market, associating reimbursement r with care recipients' health conditions. If standardized content of care were provided according to care recipients' conditions, care recipients could compare the quality of care of providers. In addition, providers could not behave opportunistically as long as the data shows, in public, the condition of the recipients they serve. The nursing homes, thus, focus on competition for better quality of care. The second modification removes price p from the existing market model. As observed earlier in this chapter, price p leaves low quality in the market, as there is always a group of people who cannot afford expensive, high quality care. If quality q is the only criterion for selecting a provider, those who care about quality naturally give nursing homes incentives to enhance quality of care, because they choose nursing homes based on quality of care. In summary, these adaptations redirect market competition away from financial competition and toward care competition, so that the competitive climate works to improve quality of care and, thereby, to eliminate poor quality of care.

The new market model presented by the author in this book is called the CMM and is distinguished from the existing market model. Unlike the existing market model, the CMM is based on a universal system. Under such a system, people co-purchase necessary long-term care and distribute it according to individual needs dictated by health conditions. Setting certain criteria for each level of care needs, the government outsources distribution to the providers in the market.

In the CMM, therefore, the providers (i.e., nursing homes) compete for a better quality of service. As for the providers' profit maximization, accepting the care recipients who need constant care certainly increases their income, but also consumes many resources (the expenses of the nursing home increases), and vice versa. As long as there is competition in the market, nursing homes with low quality of care are unlikely to be chosen by care recipients.

In the CMM, the universal long-term care insured (insurance holders[8]) i (i.e., all care recipients) care about quality. The providers, therefore, maximize profit with respect to quality of care:

$$\max_{q} \pi = ix\left(q\right) - c(q \mid \bar{x}) \tag{3}$$

where q is quality, c is cost, and $\bar{x}$ is total bed supply.

In summary, because the existing market model in the previous literature does not possess the mechanism to solve the problems in the human service market, an alternative model is necessary. The alternative is the CMM presented in this book, which directs market competition solely for better care quality.

It requires three conditions for application: (a) a universal long-term care system, (b) standardized content of care according to care recipients' conditions, and (c) no price competition.

5.   Questions about the CMM

The CMM logically solves the care quality issue in the market, because low quality of care is automatically eliminated by market competition in the model. Nevertheless, several empirical and theoretical questions remain regarding CMM. The first is its *empirical implementability*. Is it possible to meet the following requirements: (a) a universal long-term care system, (b) standardized content of care according to care recipients' condition, and (c) no price competition? Chapter 3 provides answers by investigating a case that introduces the CMM.

The second question is about the *empirical efficacy* of the CMM. The CMM assumes that all care recipients have access to a provider's care quality information and can compare providers based on their care quality. However, that assumption conflicts with information asymmetry models in the care market. That is, these models claim that care recipients do not have access to the signals of providers' care quality and thus, cannot choose a provider based on care quality. This issue is addressed in Chapter 4.

The last issue is the *financial sustainability* of the CMM. As indicated, the CMM is based on a universal system, in which governments are responsible for service provision to all people. Compared to a means-tested system, many researchers claim that a universal system is more costly, because coverage is much wider. Since the demand for human services is increasing, the CMM, based on a universal system, might not be realistic. This debate is examined in Chapter 5.

Notes

1 The reimbursement rate paid to nursing homes depends on historical costs and is independent of care recipients' health (Norton, 2000). According to Norton (2017), however, "pay for performance," the idea of paying for performance, not quantity, has lately begun to be implemented in several areas of care in some regions.
2 The benefit is a care service, not cash.
3 Recipients would care for something irrelevant to the quality of care (e.g., the beauty of the nursing home building), rather than the quality of care.
4 The term "inexpensive" might sound strange in economics, but the term is necessary to describe the *price* component in association with *quality* in the indifference curve: utility needs to be greater to the right (or the above) of the figure.
5 The cases of Canada and Australia are hard to categorize, because of huge regional differences in their systems, and the so-called "slide scale" system in Australia, by which most people are eligible for at least partial support according to income level.

6 Although the OECD consists of 31 member countries, the OECD (2005) reported only the selected 19 countries owing to lack of available data. The 19 nations included are South Korea, the Netherlands, Luxemburg, Norway, Sweden, Austria, Germany, Japan, Mexico, New Zealand, Poland, Spain, Switzerland, United Kingdom, Hungary, Ireland, United States, Australia, and Canada.

7 It is an external evaluation system. Only community-based services must receive this evaluation.

8 This indicates universally insured people, meaning those people under the universal long-term care system with taxation.

3 Verifying the implementability of the care market model

The previous chapter presented the CMM, which theoretically overcomes the tension between quality and price in human service markets. This chapter begins to test the CMM by assessing whether the three conditions for that model can be implemented. Specifically, the research underpinning this chapter examines the systems of long-term care provided across OECD nations to identify whether any existing system fulfills the three preconditions of CMM:

Condition 1: a universal long-term care system;
Condition 2: standardized content of care according to care recipients' conditions; and
Condition 3: no price competition.

An initial survey of OECD countries shows that Japan is the only country whose long-term care market fulfills all three conditions of the CMM. First, across the OECD, eight nations apply universal care systems: Austria, Germany, Japan, Luxemburg, the Netherlands, Norway, Sweden, and South Korea (see Table 2.1). Among these eight nations, only four have systems that standardize content of care according to care recipients' conditions: Germany, Luxemburg, Japan, and South Korea. Finally, among these four nations, Japan is the only country that excludes price competition in the long-term care market, and thus, is the only nation that fulfills all three of the conditions.

That Japan is applying the system supports the fact that the three preconditions of CMM are sustainable in practice. The three sections of this chapter verify in detail that each condition is fulfilled by the LTCI market in Japan. This work will contribute to the empirical implementability of the CMM.

1. Condition 1: the long-term care system in Japan is universal

The Government of Japan implemented the LTCI system of universal care in 2000, against the backdrop of rising social needs. Half the funding comes from insurance contributions and the rest from general taxes, including 25 percent

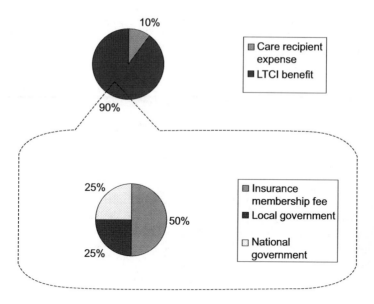

Figure 3.1 LTCI benefits and sources of funds

each from local and central governments. Those aged 40 years or above pay insurance fees according to their income.

However, the payment methods vary depending on the age of the insured. For example, the payments of category two insured people (aged 40–64 years) are from the health insurance they are subscribed to (national health insurance or their occupational medical insurance), while the payments of category one insured people (aged 65 years and above) are from the normal payments for LTCI premiums (e.g., bank transfers) or special separate payments (e.g., deductions from the pension).

Insurance holders[1] receive care when necessary. The LTCI covers 90 percent of the cost of care and the remaining 10 percent falls to the care recipients (Figure 3.1).[2] In other words, normally, by covering 10 percent of the costs, the insured can receive long-term care services according to their needs (however, high-income earners must cover 20 percent). There are two significant features of an LTCI market: (a) all organizations can enter the LTCI market as service providers as long as they register with local governments, and (b) the prices of all services in an LTCI market are publicly fixed. These characteristics are due to the government's intention to let the providers focus on competition for better service quality.

2.   Condition 2: long-term care system in Japan provides standardized content of care according to care recipients' conditions

The overview of the process to use LTCI is shown in Figure 3.2. When the need for nursing care for the insured person arises, they first apply to the

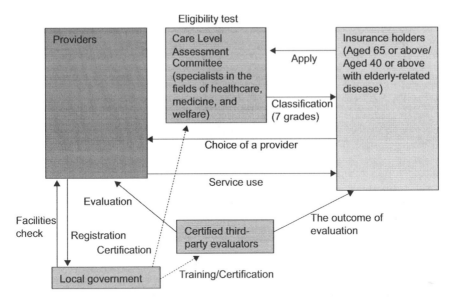

Figure 3.2 Overall process of LTCI benefits

municipality for a resident's card for an eligibility test. This test consists of three parts: (a) quantitative computer analysis based on 82 standardized criteria, (b) qualitative analysis based on interviews and observations by publicly certified investigators (*Kaigo Shien Senmon-in*), and (c) personal physicians' opinions. The results are examined by a Care Level Assessment Committee (*Kaigo Nintei Shinsa Kai*), a group of specialists in the fields of healthcare, medicine, and welfare. Then, the applicants are classified into eight evaluation categories (seven eligible categories plus one "not eligible" category), according to their needs for long-term care.

The approximate standards of these evaluation categories are seen in Table 3.1. Support 1 indicates the lightest condition, whereas Care 5 means "bed-ridden." The elderly with Care 3 or above require full ADL support and many of them suffer from dementia. As seen in Table 3.2, each category occupies approximately 8 percent–20 percent of the beneficiaries.

Those who are eligible can choose to combine a range of long-term care services. Table 3.3 indicates the benefit limit of each grade. The benefits are in-kind, not paid in cash.

There are diverse care services available in the Japanese market. Table 3.4 indicates available types of services. Users usually select a suitable type of service from the choices. For users who choose group home providers, the cost of care is shown in Table 3.5.

Table 3.1 Approximate standards of the seven grades

	Support 1	Support 2	Care 1	Care 2	Care 3	Care 4	Care 5
Grade	Needs daily methodological support to maintain their condition	Needs some assistance for daily life	Needs partial care occasionally	Needs partial care for daily life	Needs constant care	Difficult to live daily life without constant care	Not capable of spending daily life without constant care
Stand and move on foot		Needs some assistance occasionally	Needs some assistance	Needs some assistance	Needs some assistance	Not capable	Not capable
Stand up/keep standing on a single leg	Needs some assistance occasionally	Needs some assistance	Needs some assistance	Needs some assistance	Not capable	Not capable	Not capable
Excrete				Needs partial assistance occasionally	Needs partial assistance occasionally	Needs full assistance	Needs full assistance
Eat					Needs partial assistance occasionally	Needs partial assistance	Needs partial assistance
Daily routine, such as nail cutting and changing clothes	Needs partial assistance occasionally	Needs partial assistance occasionally	Needs partial assistance occasionally	Needs partial assistance	Needs full assistance	Needs full assistance	Needs full assistance
Symptoms of decreasing comprehension	Can be seen occasionally	Can be seen occasionally	Can be seen partially	Can be seen partially	Can be seen entirely	Can be seen entirely	Can be seen entirely
Abnormal behavior	Can be seen occasionally	Can be seen occasionally	Can be seen occasionally	Can be seen occasionally	Can be seen occasionally	Can be seen occasionally	Can be seen entirely

Source: Niigata City (2008)

Table 3.2 LTCI beneficiaries by grades (as of April 2006)

	Support 1	Support 2	Care 1	Care 2	Care 3	Care 4	Care 5
Ratio*	8.2%	9.1%	19.9%	18.7%	16.5%	14.6%	12.1%
Number (unit: thousand)	(206.5)	(227.2)	(499.6)	(469.8)	(413.4)	(365.7)	(303.8)
Total: 2,506							

* The rest, 0.8% (20,100), receive benefits as a care grade interim measure.

Source: MHLW (2008a: 16)

Table 3.3 Benefit limit of each grade

Grade	Monthly maximum coverage
Support 1	JPY 49,700 (USD 497)
Support 2	JPY 104,000 (USD 1,040)
Care 1	JPY 165,800 (USD 1,658)
Care 2	JPY 194,800 (USD 1,948)
Care 3	JPY 267,500 (USD 2,675)
Care 4	JPY 306,000 (USD 3,060)
Care 5	JPY 358,300 (USD 3,583)

Source: Niigata City (2008)

Table 3.4 Choice of major care services

At-home care	Institutional care
Home-visit services	**Community-based services**
• Home-help service	• Group home for the elderly with dementia
• Home-visit nursing	
• Home-visit bathing service	**Facility Services**
• Home-visit rehabilitation	• Health services facilities for the elderly
Commuting services	• Special nursing homes for the elderly
• Day care service	
• Day rehabilitation service	• Sanatorium-type medical care facilities
Short-stay services	
• Short-stay for the elderly requiring care	
• Short-stay for the elderly requiring medical care	

Notes: The names for care services are often confusing, because care services usually have two different names: the address term and law term. Special nursing homes for the elderly are *Kaigo-Roujin-Hoken-Shisetsu* (or *Tokubetsu-Yougo-Roujin-Houmu*), sometimes translated as assisted nursing homes. In addition, health service facilities for the elderly are *Kaigo-Roujin-Hoken-Shisetsu* (or *Rouken-Shisetsu*), sometimes translated as intermediate nursing homes (e.g., Sugahara, 2010).

Table 3.5 Cost of group homes for elderly with dementia

Level	Cost (per day)	Personal expense (per day)
Support 2	JPY 8,310 (USD 83.1)	JPY 831 (USD 8.31)
Care 1	JPY 8,310 (USD 83.1)	JPY 831 (USD 83.1)
Care 2	JPY 8,480 (USD 84.8)	JPY 848 (USD 84.8)
Care 3	JPY 8,650 (USD 86.5)	JPY 865 (USD 86.5)
Care 4	JPY 8,820 (USD 88.2)	JPY 882 (USD 88.2)
Care 5	JPY 9,000 (USD 90)	JPY 900 (USD 90)

Notes: Support 1 is not eligible for use for group home services. Care 2 recipients or below cannot reside at a group home.

3.   Condition 3: there is no price competition in the long-term care market in Japan

A unique feature of the LTCI in Japan is the exclusion of price competition. In the LTCI market, therefore, care is provided based on necessity, not preference. Even if economically wealthy elderly people with Care 1 want to reside at a group home, for example, they would not be allowed (see Table 3.4 for more details) when it was not necessary. In addition, care providers do not provide/receive anything other than the designated care/price.

Nevertheless, insufficient quantity of care provision automatically creates a new market with price competition outside the managed market. As discussed in Chapter 1, an important purpose of human service provision is to ensure a certain quality level. If human services provided through the managed market do not achieve this purpose, people have to look for necessary care outside the market.

In that case, the effect of no price competition in the managed market would be limited, because the markets outside the managed one would have price competition. Therefore, we need to investigate whether sufficient care is provided through the LTCI market in order to confirm whether the condition of no price competition is met. The following section investigates this, examining the possible long-term care market outside of the LTCI scheme in Japan.

4.   Market outside LTCI scheme

While several private long-term-care-related markets exist in Japan, they operate only as a supplement to the managed LTCI scheme. As for facility services, a type of provider known as an elderly home (*Keihi Roujin Houmu*) serves the semi-independent elderly in Japan (i.e., in principle, those aged 60 years and above who do not need nursing care but who cannot live at home due to their family and living situations, decline in physical functions, etc.). Elderly homes are classified into types A to C; types A and B are accommodation only, whereas type C offers meal services as well (type C is characterized by a barrier-free structure and is generally also called a care home). Although elderly homes must register with local governments to open for business, they can set their service prices freely, except for the administration fee, which is required to be progressive according to a resident's financial means.[3] However, doubts remain about whether these elderly homes provide long-term care. Although they serve the elderly in particular, they do not provide anything other than hostel-type services, such as accommodation, meals, and laundry. If care recipients (i.e., residents) require care with entitled grades, they must either move to institutional care service providers or request at-home care service providers while living at an elderly home.

Similarly, the market for home-delivery services outside the LTCI scheme cannot substitute for the LTCI scheme. Although many private companies deliver several ADL-related services, including meal delivery, personal shopping, and electric device replacement (e.g., electric bulbs) for the elderly, they do not provide "care."

As for insurance, some companies offer private LTCI, but the impact is, again, limited, for logical reasons. First, compared with the sale of other types of insurance, such as health and car, selling LTCI tends to be costly. Selling insurance becomes most attractive principally when risk is the care recipient's adverse choice. This works to sell health and car insurance because insurance holders normally try hard not to suffer from sickness or accidents. However, in the case of long-term care, the insured person's expectation of being in a nursing home is highly positively correlated with purchasing LTCI, even after controlling for observable expenditure risks, such as health status (Sloan and Norton, 1997). Insurance companies, therefore, have to invest a great amount of money to screen for bad risks. According to Norton (2000), insurance companies typically have to deny 10–20 percent of elderly applications. This screening procedure certainly adds to the burden of making profits. According to Cutler (1996), the administrative load is typically one-half to two-thirds of the total cost. High costs raise premiums, which in turn, reduces demand. For these reasons, private long-term care insurer rates in Japan are very small. The data, although a little old, are as follows: 5.4 percent for those aged in their 40s, 4.6 percent for those in their 50s, and 6.9 percent for those in their 60s or above (General Insurance Association of Japan, 2002). As a result, private LTCI occupies only 1.3 percent of the entire private insurance market in Japan (Life Insurance Association of Japan, 2002).

In summary, the private long-term care market in Japan plays only a supplemental role in the LTCI market, and both markets are uncompetitive. Therefore, in Japan, the LTCI feature that excludes price competition remains.

5.   Publishing of care quality information: the fourth CMM condition

The evidence confirms that the Japanese LTCI meets the three conditions of the CMM, but the research also highlights the importance of access to care quality information in ensuring the operation of the LTCI system. This section discusses the necessity for transparency in the dissemination of information regarding the quality of care associated with all care providers in the market. All recipients must have access to the same care quality information to support care choices. The significance of this factor suggests that access to care quality information should be established as a condition required to make the CMM work. Therefore, a fourth condition for the introduction of the CMM is that governments publish providers' care quality information.

The Japanese LTCI market has two types of provider of care-quality assurance systems: annual facility inspections by local governments and annual external evaluations by certified examiners. The facility inspection is mandatory for all providers, by which providers must meet basic requirements. Disqualified providers face punishment, including being ordered to suspend business. The external evaluation consists of three types, which are summarized in Table 3.6 and discussed below.

First, Care Service Information (CSI), which is mandatory for all providers, aims to provide users with objective information about the providers in the market. CSI provides two types of information: a basic report and a surveyed report. Whereas the basic report includes the capacity and staff allocation of a provider, the surveyed report mentions matters that are more detailed: whether or not the provider has a guideline for staff training, and whether or not the provider has a database of provided services. A significant feature of SCI is that all the included information is objective based on fact. SCI does not provide any subjective report, such as evaluating whether the guidelines are good or bad. Instead, SCI asks about facts, like whether the provider has guidelines for staff training. In this way, care recipients can obtain non-biased information on providers.

Second, third-party evaluation is available to all providers, albeit optionally. The purpose of this evaluation is to enhance providers' care quality by

Table 3.6 Care quality evaluation programs

Evaluation program	Targeted provider	Remarks
Care service information (*Kaigo saabisu johou*)	All (mandatory)	• Consists of both self-evaluation and surveyed information • Based on facts • Aims to provide non-biased information to service recipients
Third-party evaluation (*daisansha hyouka*)	All (optional)	• Aims to enhance service providers' quality through consultation
External evaluation (*gaibu hyouka*)	Group homes only (mandatory)	• Aims to evaluate service quality on behalf of frail elderly users

Source: MHLW (2008a)

professional consulting. Examining a provider's care service and managerial structure, the evaluators, licensed by the municipality, give feedback to the provider. The outcome is open to the public. However, care recipients do not usually utilize the information to compare providers, because not all providers are evaluated. Some municipalities strongly encourage providers to use the evaluation annually, but most municipalities leave it as optional.

Third, the external evaluation of care quality is mandatory for community-based service providers. Most care recipients at community-based services are dementia-suffering elderly who cannot exercise their rights as consumers. Therefore, certified external evaluators[6] assess the providers' care quality on behalf of care recipients. The care quality indicators are designed by the central government and updated every three years. The outcome is public, and care recipients are expected to use this information when choosing a provider.

While on the one hand the Japanese LTCI system implements these quality assurance systems, on the other hand, it is still cautious about measuring care quality. In fact, mandatory external evaluation of care quality is the only system that publishes care quality information in order for care recipients to choose providers. Care recipients, therefore, have access to care quality information only when choosing a community-based service provider.

There are several community-based services in the LTCI market, including group homes. However, because group homes occupy a very significant portion of community-based services, the terms "group home" and "community-based service" are often used interchangeably in this book. The rest of this chapter specifically investigates mandatory external evaluations in the Japanese group home market.

6. Mandatory external evaluation

The content of mandatory external evaluations of care quality (hereafter, mandatory external evaluations) covers a diverse field of quality of care. This evaluation system was introduced to the group home market in 2005/2006 to publish information about and enhance service quality.[7] Table 3.7 shows the index of mandatory external evaluation of service quality.

Like any other measurement, certainly, mandatory external evaluation is not an absolute indicator of quality of care. However, this evaluation covers important details of care, including some background of care implementation: life environment and managerial structure. Moreover, the items of each sub-index mention details that play an important role in ensuring the quality of long-term care, because many care recipients in the current conditions cannot always express their complaints adequately (Braithwaite, 2001). In fact, Wiener *et al.* (2007: 8), who internationally compared quality assurance for long-term care, pointed out the comprehensiveness of mandatory external evaluations, saying, "Japan appears to be the only country to have developed special approaches to assure the quality of care in facilities for people with dementia."

Table 3.7 Index of mandatory third-party evaluation[4]

Index	Sub-index
I Corporate philosophy	1) Publicity about corporate philosophy (4 items)
II Life environment	2) Homely living space (4 items)
	3) Customized living space (6 items)
III Care service	4) Care management (7 items)
	5) Basic care implementation (8 items)
	6) ADL[5] support (10 items)
	7) Life support (2 items)
	8) Medical and health support (9 items)
	9) Community life (1 item)
	10) Interaction with family (1 item)
IV Managerial structure	11) Administrative procedures (10 items)
	12) Response to complaints (2 items)
	13) Interaction between GH and family (3 items)
	14) Interaction between GH and community (4 items)

Source: Welfare and Medical Service Agency (2010a)

Note: GH indicates Group Home.

7. Chapter summary

This chapter confirmed that the CMM, presented in Chapter 2, is possible in practice by demonstrating that the conditions for implementation are met in the LTCI in Japan. Specifically the LTCI system in Japan incorporates: (a) a universal long-term care system, (b) standardized content of care according to care recipients' conditions, and (c) no price competition.

Nevertheless, in order for the CMM to work, the LTCI system must publish information on providers' care quality. Otherwise, care recipients cannot compare the care quality of providers and choose one based on its delivery of quality care. In Japan, the care quality information of all community-based services (i.e., group home) providers is publicly available. In this chapter, we have observed that publishing providers' care quality information is one of the essential prerequisites for the CMM to function.

Chapter 4 takes a further step in testing the CMM by examining whether the condition of access to quality information can resolve the problem of information asymmetry in the market.

Notes

1 The insurance holders include all care recipients in Japan aged 65 years or above plus those aged 40 years or above who suffer from elderly-related diseases, such as Alzheimer's. For those who are not eligible for LTCI but still require long-term

care, other national programs, such as handicapped care and the healthcare program, are available.

2 Care recipients with high income must pay 20 percent of the cost. As of mid-2018, care recipients with very high income must pay 30 percent of the cost.

3 The ranges of the administration fee are 0–120,000 yen [0–1,200 USD]/month for type A; 15,000–30,000 yen [150–300 USD]/month for type B; and 10,000–90,000 yen [100–900 USD]/month for type C.

4 The index has been updated gradually since 2008, but this book uses the old index, which was used mainly prior to 2008, due to data accessibility.

5 ADL means Activities of Daily Living

6 They are licensed by municipalities.

7 There was a two-year trial period prior to the introduction: providers that had already entered the market before 2005 had to disclose evaluation outcomes at least once within the trial period.

4 Verifying the implementation effects (efficacy) of the care market model

This book proposes that care users ought to be able to choose a provider based on quality of care, so that market competition sustainably enhances quality of care. In the previous chapter, we find that in the group home market, quality of care can function as the single factor in choosing a provider. Does the case of the group home market justify the validity of the CMM? If so, the case should be able to meet the following three conditions: (a) users choose a provider based on quality of care, (b) competition among providers enhances quality of care, and (c) new market entrants bring increased qualified care into the market, because they know that providers are chosen based on quality of care.

Nevertheless, in previous studies it was noted that information asymmetry exists between users and providers in the care market, which contradicts the abovementioned conditions. The following are the three models of contradictory information asymmetry.

1   the contract failure model, which claims care users perceive non-profit providers as a sign of good service quality;
2   the Medical Arms Race (MAR) model, which argues that competition in the care market tends to lower quality of care; and
3   the hypobook of Suzuki and Satake, by which services provided by new entrants in the long-term care market further raise awareness of competition from the MAR hypobook, and thus, service quality in the market as a whole deteriorates as new entrants increase in number.

This chapter, therefore, specifically verifies the validity of the three models that disagree with the CMM's achievements, investigating the outcomes of the mandatory external evaluation in the group home market in Japan.

1.   Reviewing testing models

The three models of contradictory information asymmetry on which the CMM is premised are as follows.

1.1. *Contract failure model: users cannot choose a provider based on service quality*

According to the contract failure model introduced by Hansmann (1980), in the care market, care users cannot choose a provider based on service quality, because there is information asymmetry between users and providers. Thus, users see the ownership of providers as a signal of service quality. In other words, they choose non-profit providers rather than for-profit providers whom, they believe, tend to behave opportunistically (Hansmann, 1980; Hirth, 1999).

However, this does not necessarily mean that the care quality of non-profit providers is actually better than that of for-profits (Endo, 1995; Suzuki, 2002). There are three arguments for this proposition. First, owing to the limitation of ownership, non-profits have no incentives to improve cost-effectiveness and service quality as much as for-profits do (James and Rose-Ackerman, 1986). Second, the incentive to improve service quality is difficult to identify, regardless of the ownership of providers, if the market is protected from price competition (Nanbu, 2000; Tuckman and Chang, 1988). Third, it is highly likely that the development of information technology that minimizes information asymmetry will benefit for-profit providers (Ben-Ner, 2002).

Many empirical studies have reflected this dispute. On one hand, Weisbrod (1980) and Cohen and Spector (1996) investigated the long-term care market in the United States and concluded that the service quality of non-profits was superior to that of for-profits. Gertler (1984), who also surveyed the care market in the United States, claimed the opposite. However, Nyman (1988) and O'Brien *et al.* (1983) concluded there was no significant difference. Endo (2006) argued that these different outcomes stemmed from the absence of a clear definition of service quality.

Nevertheless, the hypobook of "contract failure" could be true. Certainly, as Hansmann (1980) stated, if the service quality of non-profits were better than that of for-profits, the care recipient's "signal" would be correct. This means there would be no "contract failure." However, as seen above, the causal relationship between the provider's ownership and the service quality is still not clear.

The solution to this "contract failure" is for care recipients to be able to access service quality information from the providers. Hirth (1999) pointed out that repeat purchasing helps care recipients grasp a provider's service quality level. Although this might not be realistic in purchasing long-term care services, it is still important to fill the information gap between care recipients and providers, as information asymmetry is the condition of contract failure.

The LTCI market in Japan has been actively involved in filling the information gap. Implementing the LTCI in 2000, the Japanese government has shaped a standardized care quality measurement and built a database of evaluation outcomes. Examples of this measurement are the optional third-party evaluation system in 2003, mandatory evaluation system (*gaibu-hyoka seido*) for community services in 2005, and LTCI information disclosure system (*kaigo service johou koukai seido*) in 2007. As for the database that makes this information available to the public, the Welfare and Medical Service Network (WAM-NET) system has been operating since 2001.

The dispute over whether the ownership of providers affects care quality is evident in Japan as well. Morozumi (2007) surveyed group home providers in the Tokyo metropolitan area and Osaka city. She claimed that non-profits provided better quality care-recipient transfers than for-profits did, because of diversification. Suzuki (2002), on the other hand, surveyed at-home care providers in the Kanto area in 2001 and claimed there was no significant difference between the ownership of providers in care quality, yet 75 percent of the market share in that year was occupied by non-profits, more than for-profits, which should provide the same level of quality. Suzuki (2002) pointed out this was one type of "contract failure." Six years after Suzuki's claim, the market share of for-profits that corrected the "distortion" from this contract failure increased to nearly 50 percent. Sakurai (2008) analyzed the service quality of group home providers in Kyoto and Shiga prefectures and claimed there was still no significant difference between non-profits and for-profits in service quality; he implied that the difference in service quality between non-profits and for-profits reflected the market share (Figure 4.1). This meant there was no contract failure in the Japanese LTCI market.

This chapter is aimed at addressing two deficiencies in previous research. The first relates to the quality and quantity of the data to be analyzed. The sample

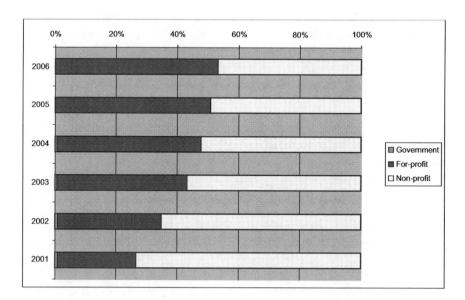

Figure 4.1 Transition of market share by type of provider (as of October in each year)

Source: MHLW (2007) and Health and Welfare Statistics Association (2007: 189–191)

size of the surveys by Morozumi (2007) and Suzuki (2002) was only a few hundred people (Suzuki: 437; Morozumi: 108), although these sizes were acceptable in the research environment at the time. Sakurai's (2008) research utilized data in only two prefectures out of 47. These outcomes have left a question about the validity of the data. The second research gap this book addresses relates to an investigation of the reasons for the dispute over whether the ownership of providers influences care quality. This chapter, therefore, analyzes the features of providers' ownership.

1.2. Medical arms race model: competition might not enhance service quality

According to the MAR model, competition in the care market tends to lower care quality. To be competitive in the market, providers spend money on advertising or renovation of buildings and equipment rather than on improving care quality itself (Hersch, 1984; Luft *et al.*, 1986; Robinson, 1988).

This model has been actively researched in the healthcare market in the United States, and many providers have acknowledged the phenomenon. Defining competitiveness as market intensity,[1] Wilson and Jadlow (1982) claimed that the more competitive a market is, the less technically efficient it is. According to Farley (1985), care tends to be expensive at hospitals in competitive markets. However, Robinson and Luft (1985) found the opposite was true. Zwanziger and Melnick (1988) claimed that the phenomenon was due to the over-prescription of hospitals in competitive markets. Devers *et al.* (2003) and Berenson *et al.* (2006) argued that over-prescription was spreading from medical treatment to the amenity of hospitals.

There are a few criticisms of the MAR model. Dranove *et al.* (1992) claimed that hospitals in competitive markets needed to respond to the need for high-tech medical treatment, introducing the latest equipment. Thus, it was natural that treatment at such hospitals cost more, and this was not a matter of inefficiency. Moreover, by defining care quality as mortality, and market competitiveness by the Herfindahl–Hirschman Index (HHI), Shortell and Hughes (1988) denied the causal relationship between care quality and the market mechanism. Kessler and McClellan (1999) also denied the hypobook of the MAR model, claiming that market competitiveness lowered the mortality rate of patients. As for the research on nursing homes in the United States, Gertler and Waldman (1992) claimed that the market mechanism enhanced service quality, while Nyman (1994) criticized the policy that regulated nursing homes' capacity in order to avoid the MAR syndrome, claiming that the policy discouraged providers' efforts to be effective.

There is little research on this issue in the Japanese LTCI market. The notable exceptions are the theoretical research of Nanbu (2000) and the empirical study of Zhou and Suzuki (2004). Pointing out that there is no price competition in the market, Nanbu (2000) discussed the possibility that market competition would lead providers to compete for better care quality, not just rent seeking and advertising. Zhou and Suzuki (2004) surveyed long-term care providers in the Kanto area in September 2001, right after the implementation of the Japanese LTCI, and claimed there was little correlation between care quality and market competitiveness.

This chapter investigates the relationship between care quality and market competitiveness many years after the implementation of the Japanese LTCI. If there were relationships between them, the research also searched for these reasons in the background to this relationship.

1.3. Suzuki and Satake's (2001) model: new market entrants might not bring better quality service

According to Suzuki and Satake's (2001) model, new entrants in the care market do not contribute to improving the market's care quality. In general, new entrants are expected to bring better quality care to the market, but in the case of the care market, they might spend resources on advertising rather than on care quality improvement. Suzuki and Satake (2001), surveying 445 at-home care providers in the Kanto area in 2000, pointed out that the advertising costs out of the total cost of new entrants is greater than that of old entrants.

Nanbu (2000) presented a different view. He assumed that new entrants entered the market with a break-even price (Ps) that was lower than that of existing providers (Pr). Thus, they might use their excess profit (Pr-Ps) for the improvement of care quality. In this case, however, Pr-Ps might still be spent on something other than care quality improvement (e.g., advertising), as Suzuki and Satake (2001) argued. This competition in advertising could drag Pr up into balance with Ps.

However, Suzuki and Satake's (2001) model still needs to be validated. The model was investigated right after the implementation of the Japanese LTCI. The existing providers at the time were dominantly non-profits, whereas the majority of new entrants were for-profits, due to the market deregulation at the time. In addition, as mentioned above, the government has attempted to solve this problem by bridging the information gap between care recipients and providers. Thus, this chapter investigates whether new entrants bring a more qualified level of care into the market today.

2. Verification method and data

In order to examine the validity of the three models presented in the previous section, this research primarily investigates the correlation between providers' quality of care (i.e., the outcome of mandatory third-party evaluation) and providers' various attributes. These attributes are the ownership for the contract failure model, the market competitiveness of the providers' located area for the MAR model, and the timing of market entry for Suzuki and Satake's (2001) model.

The data source used is the WAM-NET database[2] for group home providers in FY2006/2007.[3] The sample was 1,093 group home providers[4] in six

Table 4.1 Distribution of providers by ownership

Ownership		This research	National census
For-profit providers	Stock corporations, limited private companies	646 (60.43%)	4,417 (52.9%)
Non-profit providers	Social welfare associations	196 (18.33%)	1,826 (21.9%)
	Medical corporations	144 (13.47%)	1,554 (18.6%)
	Cooperative associations	0 (0%)	31 (0.4%)
	Civil corporations	1 (0.09%)	29 (0.3%)
	Specified NPOs	81 (7.48%)	453 (5.4%)
	Other organizations	1 (0.09%)	23 (0.3%)
Public providers	Local public organizations	0 (0%)	17 (0.2%)
	Social welfare corporations (excluding social welfare associations)	0 (0%)	0 (0%)
Total		1,069 (100%)	8,350 (100%)

Notes: The national census data are from October 2007, quoted from the MHLW (2007). The categorization of ownership is from Shimizutani and Suzuki (2002: 17). There are 24 providers missing ownership information due to a broken link; they are excluded from this table.

prefectures in the Kanto area,[5] which comprised 13 percent of all group home providers in Japan. Table 4.1 shows the distribution of providers by ownership. Although the overall distribution of this research is similar to the national census, there are slightly more for-profits and fewer medical corporations in the investigated area. This research does not investigate public providers.

Providers' quality of care is quantified by the average item-achievement rate of each sub-index in the mandatory third-party evaluation (Table 4.2). All items indicated in Table 4.2 are the standardized sub-index measurement implemented by the central government. Although municipalities might add some local items of sub-indexes to the standardized content, this research considers only a standard format in order to collect inter-prefectural data. The outcome of the mandatory third-party evaluation shows the items that a provider passes or fails with some remarks. Therefore, in this research, the achievement rate of each sub-index is calculated by the number of items a provider clears, out of the total item number(s) in the sub-index. For example, sub-index 11, administrative procedure, has ten items. If a provider clears six items out of ten, the providers obtains a 0.6 (or 60 percent) achievement rate in the sub-index. This applies to all sub-indexes. The total score of care quality (hereafter, "total score") is the average achievement rate of all 14 indexes.

In addition, this research utilizes the quality care score of the principal component. The abovementioned total score treats all sub-indexes equally. However, sub-index 3, customized living space, for example, might not be as important as sub-index 4, care management, and vice-versa. Therefore, calculating each

Table 4.2 Mandatory third-party evaluation

Index	Sub-index	Item
I Corporate philosophy	1. Publicity about corporate philosophy (4 items)	(a) Publicity (b) Clear indication (c) Staff members' tasks (d) Education
II Life environment	2. Homely living space (4 items)	(a) The atmosphere of entrance (b) The atmosphere of common place (c) The atmosphere of living room (d) Customizing own room (bedroom)
	3. Customized living space (6 items)	(a) Supportive devices (b) Layout (c) Noise proof and lighting (d) Air infiltration (e) Clock display (f) Facilities
III Care service	4. Care management (7 items)	(a) Care planning (b) Sharing care plans among staff members (c) Meeting care recipients' requests (d) Reviewing care plan (e) Care recording (f) Communication (g) Team building
	5. Basic care implementation (8 items)	(a) Respecting care recipients (b) Friendly attitude (c) Respecting care recipients' past experiences (d) Respecting care recipients' lifestyles (e) Hearing care recipients' requests (f) Respecting care recipients' independence (g) Respecting care recipients' physical freedom (h) Unlocked door policy
	6. ADL support (10 items)	(a) Hearing meal requests from care recipients (b) Eating utensils (c) Customized cooking method (d) Recording nutritional needs (e) Enjoyable cuisine (f) Customized elimination support (g) Mental aspects of elimination support (h) Customized bathing support (i) Hair/facial treatment support (j) Support for quiet sleep

Index	Sub-index	Item
	7. Life support (2 items)	(a) Management of care recipients' property
		(b) Recreation
	8. Medical and health support (9 items)	(a) Assisting medical consultation
		(b) Collaboration with medical institutions
		(c) Supporting care recipients' routine health checkups
		(d) Exercising
		(e) Troubleshooting
		(f) Assisting with dental care
		(g) Assisting with medicine taking
		(h) First aid
		(i) Policy on infection and disease
	9. Community life (1 item)	(a) Interaction with local community
	10. Interaction with family (1 item)	(a) Interaction with family
IV Managerial structure	11. Administrative procedures (10 items)	(a) Locus of responsibility
		(b) Hearing the voices of care staff members
		(c) Sufficient number of staff members
		(d) Staff training
		(e) Stress control
		(f) Application screening process
		(g) Supporting care recipients' move-out
		(h) Hygiene
		(i) Item control
		(j) Reporting and knowledge management
	12. Response to complaints (2 items)	(a) Accepting external evaluator
		(b) Establishing complaint office
	13. Interaction between group home and family (3 items)	(a) Hearing the voices of care recipients' families
		(b) Reporting to care recipients' families
		(c) Management of care recipients' financial property
	14. Interaction between group home and community (4 items)	(a) Interaction with local municipality
		(b) Interaction with local residents
		(c) Public relations
		(d) Facility sharing

Source: Welfare and Medical Service Agency (2010a)

sub-index's principle component score, this research weights the score of each sub-index. As Table 4.3 shows, the percent of variance in the primary component (i.e., component 1 in the table) is only about 20 percent and the rest is less than 10 percent each. Thus, it is certainly reasonable to clean the data by combining similar sub-indexes, such as sub-index 2, homely living space, and sub-index 3, customized living space, in order to increase the percent of the variance. This research, nevertheless, leaves all sub-indexes as they are, because they are exactly what care recipients investigate on choosing a provider. Instead of combining sub-indexes, this research uses component 1 only, multiplying the score of each sub-index by the weight of component 1 (see Table 4.4). The score of the principal component of index 1, for example, is 0.556n. The total score of the principal component is the average of each sub-index's score of principal component.

Furthermore, this research investigates the improvement of care quality. Collecting care quality information from the previous year, the research compares the yearly care quality transition of the providers. Thus, the improvement score is the subtraction of the score in the researched fiscal year from that in the previous year. Thus, numbers above 0 mean improvement and those below 0 indicate decline; the size of the number is the degree.

Table 4.3 Total variance explained

Component	Initial eigenvalues			Extraction sums of squared loadings		
	Total	% of variance	Cumulative %	Total	% of variance	Cumulative %
1	2.898	20.696	20.696	2.898	20.696	20.696
2	1.280	9.141	29.838	1.280	9.141	29.838
3	1.149	8.205	38.042	1.149	8.205	38.042
4	0.979	6.990	45.032			
5	0.973	6.947	51.979			
6	0.938	6.698	58.677			
7	0.857	6.123	64.800			
8	0.829	5.922	70.723			
9	0.785	5.609	76.332			
10	0.743	5.304	81.636			
11	0.695	4.966	86.602			
12	0.670	4.788	91.390			
13	0.621	4.432	95.822			
14	0.585	4.178	100.000			

Note: The extraction method is principal component analysis.

Table 4.4 Component matrix[a]

Sub-index	Component		
	1	*2*	*3*
1. Publicity about corporate philosophy	0.556	0.215	−0.080
2. Homely living space	0.415	−0.550	−0.067
3. Customized living space	0.435	−0.478	−0.253
4. Care management	0.474	0.200	−0.362
5. Basic care implementation	0.456	−0.328	0.178
6. ADL support	0.521	−0.090	0.115
7. Life support	0.368	0.110	0.371
8. Medical and health support	0.567	0.114	−0.296
9. Community life	0.360	−0.312	0.464
10. Interaction with family	0.275	0.102	0.552
11. Administrative procedures	0.636	0.149	−0.321
12. Response to complaints	0.251	0.455	0.168
13. Interaction between GH and family	0.381	0.426	0.115
14. Interaction between GH and community	0.498	0.051	0.088

Note: The extraction method is principal component analysis.

a Three components are extracted.

This research first investigates the contract failure model, comparing care quality between for-profit and non-profit providers. In the case of the Japanese market, for-profit provider indicates stock corporations and limited private companies, whereas non-profit provider means Social Welfare Associations, Medical Corporations, Cooperate Associations, Civil Corporations, Specified NPOs, and other non-profit organizations (e.g., voluntary associations). This research does not consider public providers that are local public organizations and social welfare corporations (excluding social welfare associations), because the sample is too small (see Figure 4.1).

With regard to the MAR model, this research measures market competitiveness by the HHI. The HHI is probably the most used measurement of market competitiveness in economic research, but up until this work, no study has applied it to the case of the Japanese LTCI market. The HHI in this research is estimated as follows. First, the market share of each provider is defined as providers' capacity divided by the whole capacity in the municipality,[6] because the occupancy rate of group homes was nearly 100 percent in the fiscal year[7] and the care fee in the market was uniformly regulated. Second, the HHI formula is applied, as follows:

$$H = \sum_{i=1}^{N} s_i^2.$$

For example, in a market in which two providers each have a 50 percent market share, the HHI equals $0.5^2 + 0.5^2 = 0.5$. Therefore, the correlation between a provider's quality of care and HHI determines the validation of the MAR model.

As for Suzuki and Satake's (2001) model, this research defines providers as new providers, first evaluated in the data collected for each fiscal year; the providers first evaluated prior to the fiscal year are old providers. The care quality comparison of the new and old providers assesses the validation of Suzuki and Satake's (2001) model.

In addition, this research utilizes some other attributes to eliminate possible data bias. First, it utilizes a subsidiary business as a provider's attribute. In the Japanese LTCI scheme, as mentioned earlier, care recipients can freely choose/ combine care services within the limit of the benefit. As shown earlier in Table 3.3 and Table 3.5, group home residents can seek additional care services, because the benefit of group home residents (i.e., grade 3 or above) is more than the group home residential fee. These care recipients with grade 3 or above might choose a group home provider based on its additional service choices, not just quality of care. Therefore, this research sets dummy variables (i.e., 1 if yes, 0 otherwise) for group home providers' major subsidized businesses: day care, community at-home care, and at-home care.

Second, we consider the provider's capacity. Although the maximum number of residents per provider is regulated (nine residents per unit and three units at most), capacity varies by provider. Residence size might affect the provider's quality of care. The collected data indicate that the maximum capacity is 28, the minimum 5, and the standard deviation is 15.4. However, considering the gap with other variables that are smaller than or equal to 1, this research converts the original data into a natural logarithm: $y = \ln(n)$, where n is capacity. If capacity is 9, then *ln* (9) is 2.20.

This research, however, does not consider the providers' rent and meal fees that are outside of the care fee regulation. Sugahara (2010) pointed out that prices of room rent and meal fees at group homes were not regulated, although he subsequently published a study rebutting this research.[8] He then claimed that care recipients might consider these prices when choosing a provider rather than the quality of care. Unlike the care fees, certainly, the price of rent and meal fees at group homes vary by provider. The room rent at some group home providers costs even more than 100,000 yen per month (MHLW, 2006b). Nevertheless, the influence of these price components is very limited. The room at a group home is almost always a studio type. Essentially, the care recipients at group homes do not need larger rooms because of their limited ADL capabilities.[9] As for meals, prices cannot be very different because of the municipality's group home facility inspection. Moreover, meal satisfaction is already taken into account as part of care quality (see the care quality criteria in Table 4.2, especially items c, d, and e in 6, ADL support). Therefore, the influence of the different prices is considered small. Table 4.5 indicates the descriptive statistics of the data used in this research.

Table 4.5 Descriptive statistics

	N	Min	Max	Mean	Std. deviation
New entrant dummy	1090	0.00	1.00	0.22	0.42
Subsidiary business dummy	1078	0.00	1.00	0.78	0.29
Day care					
Community at-home care	1078	0.00	1.00	0.02	0.14
At-home care	1078	0.00	1.00	0.01	0.12
Ownership (for-profit) dummy	1069	0.00	1.00	0.60	0.49
ln (Capacity)	1070	1.61	3.33	2.65	0.42
HHI	1076	0.01	1.00	0.22	0.25
New entrant dummy 2005/2006	407	0.00	1.00	0.86	0.34
Total service quality score	1093	0.47	1.00	0.92	0.08
Total service quality score of principle component	1093	0.23	0.51	0.47	0.04
Improvement service quality score	409	−0.35	0.37	0.06	0.08
Improvement service quality score of principal component	409	−0.17	0.18	0.03	0.04

Note: The sample number of improvement scores is small because many providers failed to disclose the evaluation outcome through WAM-NET in FY2005/2006, the initial year of the annual mandatory third-party evaluation system. The Ministry of Health, Labor and Welfare (MHLW) later urged municipalities to instruct providers to disclose these data within the fiscal year (MHLW, 2006a).

3. Results

3.1. *Contract failure model is not supported*

According to the contract failure model, care recipients in the care market do not choose care providers based on care quality owing to the information asymmetry between care recipients and providers. Specifically, according to Hansmann (1980), care recipients tend to choose non-profit providers, because they assume that non-profit care quality is better than for-profit care quality. This argument has provoked controversy among researchers. Therefore, the first part of this section investigates the assumption of non-profits' superiority and the contract failure hypobook. Then, the latter part of the section further discusses the causes of the disputes in previous literature by describing the implications of the investigation.

Table 4.6 employs the 14 sub-indexes in Table 4.2 to present the mean scores by ownership of two types of providers (for-profit and non-profit). This study prepares two sets of scores to measure quality of care. As explained earlier in this chapter, the total score is simply the average achievement rate of all 14 indexes. The total improvement score is the subtraction of the total score in

Table 4.6 Comparison of service quality by ownership of providers

		For-profit	*Non-profit*	*Simple*	*Controlled*
1	Publicity about corporate philosophy	0.87(0.19)	0.88(0.19)		
2	Homely living space	0.94(0.14)	0.94(0.13)		
3	Customized living space	0.95(0.11)	0.95(0.10)		
4	Care management	0.90(0.16)	0.91(0.15)		
5	Basic care implementation	0.95(0.10)	0.96(0.08)	N**	N*
6	ADL support	0.95(0.08)	0.95(0.09)		
7	Life support	0.91(0.19)	0.92(0.18)		
8	Medical and health support	0.92(0.11)	0.93(0.10)	N*	N*
9	Community life	0.95(0.22)	0.94(0.23)		
10	Interaction with family	0.98(0.13)	0.99(0.08)		
11	Administrative procedures	0.89(0.13)	0.92(0.11)	N**	N**
12	Response to complaints	0.95(0.15)	0.95(0.15)		
13	Interaction between group home and family	0.94(0.16)	0.92(0.17)	F**	F*
14	Interaction between group home and community	0.77(0.26)	0.80(0.24)	N*	
	Total score (average score of all indexes)	0.92(0.08)	0.93(0.07)		
	Score of the principal component	0.47(0.04)	0.47(0.04)		
	Improvement score (average improvement score of all indexes)	0.05(0.08)	0.06(0.08)		
	Improvement score of the principal component	0.03(0.02)	0.03(0.02)		

Note: Numbers in brackets indicate standard deviation.

* and ** mean 5% and 1% significance levels, respectively.

FY2005/2006 from that in FY2006/2007. Thus, numbers above 0 mean improvement and those below 0 indicate decline; the size of the number is the degree. The principal component score and principal component improvement score are estimated by principal component analysis, in which each index is evaluated with different weights. Furthermore, in the column of the t-test and multiple regression analysis, F indicates that the score of for-profits is significantly higher than the score for non-profits, while N denotes the reverse.

First, we consider the overall difference between for-profits and non-profits. For-profit providers and non-profit providers have an average achievement score of 0.92 and 0.93, respectively. The score of non-profit providers is slightly higher than that of for-profit ones, but the difference is not statistically significant. This also holds for the principal component score. In addition, because the improvement scores are similar, the outcome does not seem to be temporal. There is, thus, no significant difference in service quality between for-profits and non-profits.

However, this simple comparison could be misleading, because providers' other variables were not controlled. Thus, this research investigates the following variables of the providers: (a) HHI as market environment, (b) subsidiary businesses, and (c) timing of market entry (regardless whether the providers newly entered the market).[10] Table 4.7 illustrates the distribution of these variables by ownership. For-profit providers appear to accommodate more care recipients, have day service as a subsidiary business, and have more entrants that are new.

Table 4.8 shows the outcomes of the multiple regression analysis with the dependent variables as the care quality total score and principal component score, respectively. The ownership dummy does not statistically affect either total score or score of the principal component (total score: p value = 0.319 > 0.05; score of the principal component: p value = 0.236 > 0.5). This means, contrary to Hansmann's (1980) argument, there is still no significant difference in the care quality between for-profits and non-profits.

The difference in the care quality by ownership appears to be reasonable. The comparison of for-profits and non-profits in care quality indicates the

Table 4.7 Distribution by ownership of providers

		For-profits	*Non-profits*
Sample		646	423
Market environment	Herfindahl–Hirschman Index of the market (average)	0.2186	0.2133
Subsidiary business	Day service	63 (10%)	21 (5%)
	Community at-home care service	18 (3%)	3 (1%)
	At-home care service	14 (2%)	1 (0%)
Timing of market entry	New entrant	167 (26%)	75 (18%)
Size	Capacity (average)	15.70	14.95

Table 4.8 Influence of other variables

Dependent variable		Total score	Score of the principal component
		Std. coefficients (p value)	Std. coefficients (p value)
Market environment	Herfindahl–Hirschman Index	−0.092 (0.003**)	−0.090 (0.004**)
Subsidiary business	Day service dummy (1=yes, 0=otherwise)	0.071 (0.038*)	0.071 (0.037*)
	Community at-home care service dummy (1=yes, 0=otherwise)	−0.016 (0.673)	−0.017 (0.653)
	At-home care service dummy (1=yes, 0=otherwise)	−0.038 (0.309)	−0.040 (0.284)
Timing of market entry	New entrant dummy (1=new, 0=otherwise)	−0.093 (0.003**)	−0.093 (0.003**)
Size	ln (capacity)	−0.045 (0.139)	−0.044 (0.152)
Ownership	Ownership dummy (1=for-profit, 0=non-profit)	−0.031 (0.319)	−0.037 (0.236)
Adj. R^2		0.016	0.016

difference in market share, which represents the care recipients' choice, as Figure 4.1 shows. As a result, the market contained no contract failure.

However, it is too early to conclude that care recipients in the market chose a provider based on its care quality, as the variables related to the care recipients' choice, other than ownership, need to be controlled. More importantly, many of the care recipients in FY2006/2007 might not even have been able to choose a provider owing to excess demand over supply in the market. In fact, almost all group home providers in the market were fully occupied through the year (see endnote 7). As Figure 4.1 shows, more for-profits entered the market. Many care recipients chose for-profits simply because they were the only available group home providers. Therefore, it might be necessary to wait until the market provides sufficient supply over demand before drawing conclusions that contract failure exists.

This study examines the controversy of this contract failure model in the existing literature, looking at the feature of service quality by ownership. The right column of Table 4.6 shows whether there is a difference in the service quality between for-profits and non-profits, with other variables controlled by the multiple regression analysis and each index as a dependent variable.

The result is characteristic. Whereas non-profits are superior in the indexes relating directly to the care recipients, including "basic care implementation," "medical and health support," and "internal management structure," for-profits are superior to non-profits with regard to nursing homes and families. Relations with families is selected as an evaluation criteria because there are many opportunities for families to represent the voice of care recipients whose autonomy has been impaired,[11] and thus, it seems for-profits are more sensitive to the voices of the families of independent care recipients.

The above-described points clarified in this study suggest it is possible that these characteristic differences between for-profits and non-profits are the cause of the disputes in the previous literature. In other words, depending on the viewpoint, both types of ownership could perform better. Morozumi (2007), for example, preferred non-profits, assessing their service quality from care recipients' viewpoints only. Suzuki (2002), on the other hand, claimed that for-profits were possibly superior, including with respect to information disclosure[12] in the index of service quality. Result 2 for the MAR model was not supported.

3.2. *MAR model was not supported*

According to the MAR model, market competitiveness lowers care quality. This section first presents the measurement of market competitiveness, and then compares care quality between providers in competitive markets and those in non-competitive markets. Lastly, the section discusses the implications of the outcomes.

Although negative causal relationships between HHI and care quality have already been shown in Table 4.8, this section further investigates the impact, categorizing the providers into two groups: those with HHI of 0.1 or below are the competitive market, and those with HHI of 0.18 or above are the non-competitive market.[13]

Table 4.9 illustrates the description of each market. The competitive market has more new providers. The capacity of the providers in the competitive market is greater.

Table 4.10 presents the mean scores of care quality indexes by providers' market competitiveness. The principal component score and principal component improvement score are estimated by different weights based on principal component analysis. The independent-samples t-test compares both markets in the "simple" column. Furthermore, in addition to the comparison from the t-test, the market differences from the multiple regression analysis with each item as the dependent

Table 4.9 Distribution by market competitiveness of providers

		Competitive	Non-competitive
Sample		435	426
Ownership	For-profit	256 (59%)	252 (59%)
Subsidiary business	Day service	32 (7%)	44 (10%)
	Community at-home care service	9 (2%)	12 (3%)
	At-home care service	9 (2%0	6 (1%)
Timing of market entry	New entrant	119 (27%)	73 (17%)
Size	Capacity (average)	16.1	14.7

variable indicate whether there is a significant effect on the item's evaluation. C indicates that the score of the providers in the competitive market is significantly higher than that of non-profits, while N refers to the reverse.

The outcome described in this section shows that the overall care quality of providers in a competitive market (hereafter "competitive") is significantly better than providers in a non-competitive market (hereafter "non-competitive"). The total score is 0.94 for competitive and 0.91 for non-competitive; the score for competitive is higher than that for non-competitive and the difference is statistically significant. This is also the case for the score of the principal component. The result, therefore, fails to support the hypobook of the MAR model.

The MAR model suggests that market competition lowers service quality. Some critics of the MAR model argue there is little incentive to improve service quality

Table 4.10 Comparison of care quality by market competitiveness of providers

		Competitive	Non-competitive	Simple	Controlled
1	Publicity about corporate philosophy	0.91 (0.16)	0.85 (0.20)	C**	C*
2	Homely living space	0.95 (0.13)	0.93 (0.15)	C**	
3	Customized living space	0.97 (0.09)	0.95 (0.12)	C**	
4	Care management	0.93 (0.13)	0.89 (0.16)	C**	C*
5	Basic care implementation	0.97 (0.10)	0.94 (0.07)	C**	
6	ADL support	0.96 (0.07)	0.95 (0.08)	C*	
7	Life support	0.94 (0.16)	0.90 (0.20)	C**	
8	Medical and health support	0.94 (0.09)	0.91 (0.11)	C**	
9	Community life	0.96 (0.19)	0.94 (0.24)		C*
10	Interaction with family	0.99 (0.10)	0.99 (0.12)		
11	Administrative procedures	0.92 (0.11)	0.89 (0.14)	C**	
12	Response to complaints	0.96 (0.14)	0.95 (0.15)		
13	Interaction between group home and family	0.95 (0.14)	0.92 (0.18)	C**	C*
14	Interaction between group home and community	0.81 (0.24)	0.75 (0.26)	C**	
	Total score (average score of all indexes)	0.94 (0.07)	0.91 (0.07)	C**	C**
	Score of the principal component	0.48 (0.19)	0.46 (0.04)	C**	C**
	Improvement score (average improvement score of all indexes)	0.04 (0.08)	0.07 (0.08)	N**	
	Improvement score of the principal component	0.02 (0.01)	0.04 (0.02)	N**	

Note: Numbers in brackets indicate standard deviation.

* and ** mean 5% and 1% significance level, respectively.

in the non-competitive market, but they are not correct. The improvement score describes the transformation of the service quality of the providers for the two years for which the data are available (FY2005/2006 and FY2006/2007). The scores of competitive and non-competitive are 0.04 and 0.07, respectively. Both numbers are positive, which indicates improvement of care quality. This is also the case for the improvement score of the principal component.

"Competitive" (the providers in competitive markets) appears to excel, especially in the indexes related to public relations, such as corporate philosophy, community life, and interaction between the group home and the family. Their strength extends to the categories of "life environment" and "care service." This chapter presents the first empirical study of MAR with the HHI and a comprehensive service quality evaluation in the long-term care market. The outcome indicates that the mandatory third-party evaluation that makes a provider's service quality information available to the public is very useful to prevent MAR syndrome, which is caused by the information gap between care recipients and providers.

This minimized information gap creates an incentive for "non-competitive" (the providers in non-competitive markets) to enhance care quality. As Table 4.10 shows, the average improvement score of non-competitive is even higher than that of competitive. As a result, the mandatory external evaluation enhances the service quality of the market.

3.3.   *Suzuki and Satake's (2001) model was partly supported*

Suzuki and Satake's (2001) model assumes that new entrants do not enhance service quality in the care market. To investigate the validity of this assumption, this research defines providers that were first evaluated in FY2006/2007 as new entrants and those first evaluated prior to FY2006/2007 as old ones. This section presents a comparison between them and the implications from the model.

Table 4.11 illustrates the distribution of the variables of new and old entrants. New entrants tend to enter more competitive markets. Old entrants are more likely to have day care services as subsidiary businesses.

Table 4.12 indicates the mean scores of service quality indexes by the timing of market entry of the providers. The principal component score and principal component improvement score are estimated by different weights

Table 4.11 Distribution by market entry of providers

		New	*Old*
Sample		241	849
Subsidiary business	Day service	10 (4%)	74 (9%)
Market environment	Community at-home care service	3 (1%)	12 (1%)
	At-home care service	0 (0%)	4 (0%)
	Herfindahl–Hirschman Index	0.17	0.23
Size	Capacity (average)	15.1	15.5
Ownership (for-profit dummy)		164 (68%)	481 (57%)

Table 4.12 Comparison of service quality by market entry of providers

		New	*Old*	*Simple*	*Controlled*
1	Publicity about corporate philosophy	0.86 (0.19)	0.88 (0.19)		
2	Homely living space	0.93 (0.15)	0.94 (0.13)		
3	Customized living space	0.87 (0.13)	0.92 (0.10)	O*	O**
4	Care management	0.95 (0.18)	0.95 (0.15)	O*	O**
5	Basic care implementation	0.95 (0.10)	0.95 (0.09)		
6	ADL support	0.95 (0.08)	0.95 (0.08)		
7	Life support	0.92 (0.19)	0.92 (0.19)		
8	Medical and health support	0.90 (0.12)	0.93 (0.10)	O**	O**
9	Community life	0.95 (0.23)	0.95 (0.23)		
10	Interaction with family	0.99 (0.11)	0.99 (0.12)		
11	Administrative procedures	0.89 (0.13)	0.90 (0.13)		
12	Response to complaints	0.93 (0.17)	0.95 (0.14)	O*	O**
13	Interaction between group home and family	0.90 (0.19)	0.94 (0.15)		O**
14	Interaction between group home and community	0.75 (0.27)	0.79 (0.25)		O*
	Total score (average score of all indexes)	0.91 (0.09)	0.93 (0.07)	O**	O**
	Score of the principal component	0.46 (0.05)	0.47 (0.04)	O**	O**
	Improvement score (average improvement score of all indexes)	–	0.06 (0.03)	–	–
	Improvement score of the principal component	–	0.02 (0.01)	–	–

Note: Numbers in brackets indicate standard deviation.

*and **mean 5% and 1% significance levels, respectively.

Table 4.13 Comparison of care quality improvement by market entry of providers

	New	*Old*	*Simple*	*Controlled*
Improvement score (average improvement score of all indexes)	0.06 (0.03)	0.02 (0.02)	N**	N**
Improvement score of the principal component	0.03 (0.02)	0.01 (0.01)	N**	N**

Note: Numbers in brackets indicate standard deviation.

*and **mean 5% and 1% significance levels, respectively.

based on principal component analysis. Furthermore, in addition to the comparison from the t-test, the market differences from the multiple regression analysis with each item as the dependent variables indicates whether there is a significant effect on the item's evaluation. N indicates that the score of the new entrants is significantly higher than that of non-profits, whereas O refers to the reverse.

The total score in Table 4.12 is 0.91 for new entrants and 0.93 for old entrants. The score of old entrants is slightly higher than that of new entrants, and the difference is statistically significant. This is also the case for the principal component score. The outcomes, thus, support the hypobook of Suzuki and Satake's (2001) model.

Suzuki and Satake (2001) also suggested that new entrants spend their "excess profit" not on improving service quality, but on something else, like advertising. To investigate the validity of this explanation, Table 4.13 presents the transformation of the service quality of the "old" providers for which data are available for both years (FY2006/2007 and FY2005/2006). Moreover, among them, this study redefines the providers that entered the market in FY2005/2006 as "new" entrants and the rest as "old" entrants, so that the improvement of new and old entrants can be compared. However, Table 4.13 shows that new entrants improved care quality better than old ones, as Nanbu (2000) suggested.

The results demonstrate that new entrants do not bring competitive care quality into the market. However, they do improve care quality, possibly spending excess profit on that improvement.

The score of each index in Table 4.12 describes the features by the timing of market entry. It appears that the old entrants perform better in the sub-indexes in the index[14] of "management structure," such as information, consultations, and complaints, interaction between the group home and the family, and interaction between the group home and community. On the other hand, in the category of "care service," there is, with the exception of medical and health support, very little difference between new and old entrants. This implies that experience is more important in the management-structure aspect of long-term care.

4.   Summary of chapter

In order to investigate the empirical workability of the CMM, this chapter examined the validity of three care-market information asymmetry models that conflict with CMM. These information asymmetry models are (a) the contract failure model, (b) the MAR model, and (c) Suzuki and Satake's (2001) model. The analysis was based on an examination of 1,093 group home providers' care quality data in the long-term care market in Japan.

This chapter presented three major empirical findings. First, non-profits did not offer superior care quality in the market. The preference in care quality might vary depending on the viewpoint. In other words, care recipients might prefer the care of non-profits, whereas the family might choose for-profits as they place more emphasis on interaction with the family. However, the overall difference in care quality between for-profits and non-profits was not statistically significant. Second, the disclosure system of providers' care quality information bridged the care information gap between care recipients and providers, which led to enhanced care quality through market competition. Third, although new market entrants were inferior to old entrants (existing providers) in care quality, the improvement of new entrants in the following year was greater than that of old entrants. The challenge of new entrants was rather the management structure of care than care itself.

In conclusion, none of the three models tested was fully supported. The three hypobooks, which were derived on the assumption that of information asymmetry between service providers and users, at the very least are not consistent with the results of the analysis of the data on the group home market in Japan. Of course, it is difficult to conclude that information asymmetry does not exist in the Japanese long-term care market from this analysis alone, but the attempt by the Japanese government to publish information can, at the very least, be considered to a certain extent as playing a role in preventing the establishment of a market failure model that assumes information asymmetry. With regard to the proposal for a new care market model, the analysis in this book at the very least can show that information asymmetry between the service provider and consumers is not an inevitable assumption. In other words, as indicated by the model in Chapter 3, it is highly likely that group home providers compete with each other for better care quality.

$$\max_{q} \pi = hx(q) - c(q \mid \bar{x}). \tag{3}$$

Therefore, the efficacy of the CMM was to a certain extent proven in the case of a group home market that meets the conditions to implement the CMM, along with the care quality evaluation system.

In addition, this chapter justified the importance of measuring and publishing providers' care quality. According to the three information asymmetry models tested, care recipients cannot compare providers' care quality and make their choice accordingly. However, the investigations of this chapter indicate the possibility that models that assume information asymmetry do not fully function when governments measure and publish providers' care quality information.

Therefore, publishing care-quality information becomes a fourth condition to introduce the CMM. Now, the conditions of the CMM are (a) a universal long-term care system, (b) standardized content of care according to care recipients' conditions, (c) no price competition, and (d) publishing providers' care quality evaluation.

This indicates that all other long-term care markets, including Japanese at-home care and institutional care, should meet these conditions to solve the long-term care quality issue, directing market competition to enhance providers' care quality by CMM.

Notes

1 The intensity of competitiveness was measured by (referral) radius × (hospital density) × (population density) (Wilson and Jadlow, 1982: 477).
2 WAM-NET is a search engine of long-term care providers run by the Social Welfare and Medicaid Agency.
3 The data for FY2007/2008, the latest year in which this study was conducted, were not available in a uniform way, because the evaluation criteria in many prefectures were modified during the year.
4 This included all the group home providers in the market at the time.
5 The Tokyo metropolitan area is not included in this research because its care quality evaluation is exceptionally different from that of other prefectures.
6 Because group home is categorized as a community-based care service in Japan (MHLW, 2006a), it can be assumed that the market of group home providers indicates the municipal area.
7 The average number of group home care recipients (excluding short-term care recipients) in Japan in FY2006/2007 was 119,433.3 per month (MHLW (2008a: 95), less than the capacity of whole group home providers (as of October 2006) of 123,580 (MHLW, 2007). This indicates about a 97 percent occupancy rate through the year.
8 The empirical part of this chapter has already been published (Kadoya, Y., 2010, Managing the Long-Term Care Market: The Constraints of Service Quality Improvement, *Japanese Journal of Health Economics and Policy*, Vol. 21 (E1): 247–264). Corresponding to the paper, Sugahara wrote an article titled "Invited Counter Argument for Managing the Long-Term Care Market."
9 The residents of a group home are at grade 3 or above (see Table 4.3 for details).
10 The providers that participated in the mandatory third-party evaluation for the first time in FY2006/2007 are defined as new entrants.
11 Group home residents must hold care level 3 or above.
12 This includes issuing a newsletter for the members (care recipients' families).
13 According to Parkin and Bade (2006), HHI of 0.18 or above indicates concentration (i.e., low competition), whereas HHI of 0.1 or below means deconcentration (i.e., high competition).
14 There are four indexes for the sub-indexes, as seen in Table 4.2.

5 Verifying the financial sustainability of the care market model

The previous chapter concluded that all long-term care markets ought to aim to introduce the CMM in order to solve the long-term care quality issue. However, this implementation requires several conditions: (a) a universal long-term care system, (b) standardized content of care according to care recipients' conditions, (c) restricting price competition, and (d) publishing providers' care quality evaluation.

This chapter discusses the claims of the CMM from the perspective of financial sustainability to demonstrate it is not merely an impractical, armchair theory. Among these claims, while citing the CMM conditions, the universal care system, which is often criticized for being too costly, is considered.

1. Financial burden and universal care

Universal care is not necessarily costly. Normally, one can assume that universal care costs more than means-tested care. The number of universal care recipients is certainly many times greater than that of means-tested care, as universal care is for everyone, but means-tested care is for the economically vulnerable only. Assuming that the economically vulnerable account for 20 percent of the total population, then the care granted to the economically vulnerable is granted only to those within this 20 percent. On the other hand, universal care is granted to everyone, or 100 percent of the total population, which is five times as many care recipients. If there are five times as many recipients, the costs will also be five times higher, and thus, in general, it is considered that many governments have hesitated to introduce universal care because of concerns about financial sustainability.

However, in fact, the public costs in countries that have adopted universal care are not necessarily that great compared to the public costs in countries that provide care only to the economically vulnerable. While the data are a little old, Figure 5.1 plots the expenditure of public long-term care as a percentage of GDP on the Y-axis, and the share of very old people in the population (80 years and older) on the X-axis, the letter "U" in brackets indicates universal care, whereas "M" indicates care only for the economically vulnerable (means-tested). Of course, there are to a greater or lesser extent differences in the definition of

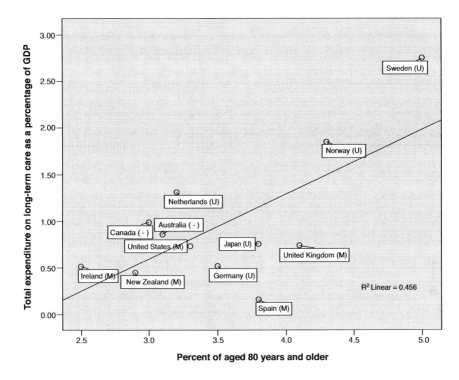

Figure 5.1 Correlation between public long-term care spending and population share of very old people (aged 80+)

Source: Figures 1.1 and 1.2, and Table 1.2

"long-term care" depending on the country, and there is some variation in the aggregate totals for the fiscal year of each country in the OECD data, which are the source of the data for the vertical axis. Therefore, the numerical values in this figure are guidelines only. However, as can be understood at a glance, "U" countries do not necessarily spend more than "M" countries do. For example, the costs of Japan (U) and Germany (U) are less than the average, whereas that of Ireland (M) is above the average. Certainly, the results for Sweden and Spain are relatively close to expectations. However, with regard to Spain, the main reason is considered to be that at the time the data on this country were collected, there had been a slight delay in its development of a public long-term care system (Sweden's high public costs are discussed later). As just mentioned, assuming that the economically vulnerable constitute 20 percent of the total population, when adopting a system of universal care, as the number of care recipients will be five times greater than if only the economically vulnerable were to receive care, it is estimated that public costs will also be approximately five times higher. However, in fact, far from being five times higher, there is practically no difference between the two. Why is this?

The reason is not because the comparatively low public costs incurred by countries adopting a universal care system do not shift the burden onto private expenditure. In the universal care system, the responsibility for the minimum necessary long-term care is essentially placed on public expenditure, and so instead, it greatly reduces private expenditure on long-term care. Table 5.1 indicates the ratio of private expenditure in the total long-term care expenditure. The average private expenditure ratio of countries with a universal care system is much lower than the ratios of the others, and as a whole, is more efficient.

The reason that long-term care expenditure in countries adopting the universal care system is more efficient is the utility resulting from economies of scale. Table 5.2 shows the size of the income gap in various countries, from data aggregated by the World Bank at the same time as the data shown in Figure 5.1. The larger the value of the Gini coefficient, the greater is the income gap, while the top 10 percent shows the percentages of total wealth possessed by the top

Table 5.1 Ratio of private expenditure to total long-term care expenditure (%)

Universal		Means-tested		Other	
Sweden	5	Ireland	16	Canada	2
Japan	8	New Zealand	34	Australia	28
Netherlands	9	United Kingdom	35		
Norway	14	United States	42		
Germany	3	Spain	73		
Average	**7.8**	**Average**	**40**	**Average**	**15**

Source: Figure 5.1

Table 5.2 The Gini coefficient and market type

	Gini coefficient (%)	Highest 10% (%)	Market
Japan	24.9	21.7	U
Sweden	25	22.2	U
Norway	25.8	23.4	U
Germany	28.3	22.1	U
Netherlands	30.9	22.9	U
Spain	32.5	25.2	M
Canada	33.1	25.0	–
Australia	35.2	25.4	–
Ireland	35.9	27.6	M
United Kingdom	36	28.5	M
New Zealand	36.2	27.8	M
United States	40.8	29.9	M

Source: World Bank (2005)

10 percent in terms of income. It is extremely interesting that the countries are cleanly divided by income gap, with countries with relatively small income gaps adopting the universal care (U) system, and those with relatively large income gaps adopting the system of care for the economically vulnerable only (M). In other words, in countries with a small income gap, because to a certain extent the level of long-term care services that people want has been settled, the governments are able to concentrate their investment of resources into realizing the provision of services at this level (facilitating economies of scale). On the other hand, in countries with large income gaps, as there is considerable divergence between the level of long-term care services demanded by the high-income group and the low-income group, the governments are unable to concentrate their resources into providing services of a certain level (economies of scale are not facilitated), and efficiency deteriorates. It is considered that as a result of this difference in efficiency, there is only a small difference between public long-term care expenditure in countries with a universal care system and countries with a system of care for the economically vulnerable only.

Then, why does Sweden, the outlier mentioned earlier, have comparatively high public expenditure, despite having a small income gap? There are probably several reasons for this, but here, an important one is considered the utility of economies of scale. At the time the data were collected, Sweden (and also Norway) were known to be extremely advanced countries in terms of the decentralization of public long-term care. Because of decentralization, even though the income gap between all citizens is small, the content of the care differs greatly depending on the requirements according to regional characteristics, and thus, it seems that the government is not able to concentrate its resources, making it difficult for economies of scale to work. Certainly, it must be noted that since the progress made in decentralization in welfare cannot be simply quantified, it is difficult to prove this argument. However, as it long has not been proven in some form that the labor productivity of Sweden's long-term care providers is not extremely low compared to other countries, it would seem logical to presume that Sweden's decentralization of long-term care provision has damaged the utility provided by economies of scale.

2. Why economies of scale are important

The previous section described how economies of scale are extremely important for a universal long-term care system from the viewpoint of efficiency. In this section, the reason for this is examined in detail, starting with the economic meaning of providing universal benefits for long-term care services.

First, in economics, long-term care can be categorized as a private good, not a public good. A public good is that which is non-rivalled and non-excludable, whereas a private good is the opposite. Non-rivalled means that consumption of the good by one individual does not reduce availability of the good for consumption by others, and non-excludable means that no one can be effectively excluded from using the good. In the real world, there might be no such thing as an absolutely non-rivalled and non-excludable good, but economists consider that some goods approximate the concept closely enough for the analysis to be economically useful. For example, if one citizen is secured by the national defense, the security of the national defense is still available for others in the country and it is very difficult to exclude anyone from the security of the country; thus, it is a non-rivalled and excludable public good. Conversely, eating a cake reduces the amount of cake available to others and people can be effectively excluded from eating the cake; therefore, a cake is a private good. Likewise, so is long-term care a private good.[1] Conversely, a public good cannot exclude a free rider. In other words, this means the government does not necessarily provide long-term care in the model, because it is not a public good. In fact, many countries basically entrust the provision of long-term care to the freely competitive market, and their governments provide care only to the economically vulnerable.

However, as the social structure has changed, governments have begun to provide many non-public goods (i.e., private goods), with the concept of merit goods. A merit good, introduced by Musgrave (1957, 1959), is a good that is judged as necessary for an individual or society based on a norm other than respecting consumer preferences. In other words, a merit good is a non-public good that is important for a government region (a country in most cases), but can also be considered a shared benefit for society as a whole.

In some countries, long-term care has become a good that benefits society, in that it is jointly purchased and shared by the members of society. Universal care is the adoption of this system. The benefits for society are that the returns are greater than the amount invested through the joint purchase of the good by society as a whole. Through the utility of economies of scale from the joint purchase, the marginal utility of the production factors is greatly improved at a certain point. If speaking of a production system of fixed inputs and variable inputs (e.g., the full capacities of facilities and care workers), then beyond a certain point, each time the variable input is increased by one unit, the output improves dramatically, and the cost of the variable input for each additional unit becomes increasingly smaller. Accompanying this phenomenon, for the first time, society recognizes long-term care as a good for which there is merit in purchasing jointly.

3. The unity of goods and income gap

The unity of goods is essential in order to obtain the utility of economies of scale, because if the goods produced are not the same, the marginal utility will not be significantly improved by mass production. This point, from the perspective of necessity, can also explain why there are examples of failures in the provision of merit goods, even though they have very large merits that are shared by society. First, the most easy-to-understand example of failure is food. Food is necessary for every member of society. Therefore, many societies throughout history have used a universal system for the food market and attempted to jointly purchase food and distribute it to members of society. However, normally, each individual has unique food preferences. Some people like rice, others like bread; some people like beef, others like chicken. Therefore, a universal system for food cannot obtain the utility from economies of scale and these attempts have almost always ended in failure, except for exceptional periods of food shortages following natural disasters and wars. On the other hand, primary education is a good that functions comparatively well as a merit good. The purpose of primary education is to share among all members of society a common body of knowledge, such as basic social norms, like reading, writing, and calculation, so the educational content is unified. Therefore, a universal system for primary education receives the utility from economies of scale and in fact, is a system that functions in many countries.

Starting with long-term care, disparity in wealth damages the integrity (unity) of human services. Generally, services that the rich want are greatly different to those that the poor want. The rich want luxurious and attentive services, while the poor want frugal and simple services. Demand for goods is diversified as the gap between rich and poor grows larger, while by contrast, when the gap is small, it becomes easier to set services at a fixed level that everyone agrees on and goods can be unified. As indicated above, this factor causes the effective and efficient spread of long-term care in countries adopting the universal system.

This finding has a number of implications for the sustainability of the provision of human services. Specifically, in order to create a sustainable human service market that reduces the financial burden on society, first, it is necessary to minimize the income gap between the rich and poor in society. Conversely, if this cannot be achieved, at the very least, the merits of introducing a universal care system disappear.

For example, in the United States in recent years, the major controversy sparked by the reforms to the medical insurance system to establish a (sort of) "universal" care system (known as Obama Care) seem related to the fact that the United States has a major income gap. Of course, as pointed out by Yamagishi (2014) and Amano (2014), to a certain extent, it is true that, considering the history of the United States and the ideals of its founding fathers, this controversy would seem to be a unique phenomenon to the United States. However, it is worth noting that in the United States in the 1960s, when the income gap was much smaller than it is today, while it had an age limit, the Medicare system was established without much resistance; Medicare was a public medical insurance system with even more of an aspect of universal care than in Obama Care once certain conditions were cleared.

In addition, the point that it is possible for the income gap between regions to grow because of decentralization gives some extremely interesting suggestions for the debate on regional creation and decentralization in the future. In the case of Sweden, while the income gap between rich and poor is small for the country as a whole, it is possible that decentralization will cause the gap between the richer and poorer regions to widen. As tax revenue is high in regions where many rich people live and in regions where large companies are located, these regions can utilize the merits of decentralization and provide attentive services, but other regions will be able to provide only simple services. When services are lacking in unity in this way, they cannot receive the utility of economies of scale and as a result, the cost as a whole becomes higher.

4.   Quality improvements in a care system only for the economically vulnerable

The previous section explained that universal care as a basis for the CMM is difficult to implement in a market with a large income gap. Certainly, all markets should intend to apply a universal system in order to implement a CMM that solves long-term care quality issues. Nevertheless, reducing the income gap normally requires a long time, and during this period, the problem of low-quality long-term care will continue. Therefore, in this section, we discuss a method for improving the quality of services that, as much as possible, will not incur costs, while maintaining care for the economically vulnerable only.

4.1.   Improving the model that assumes care only for the economically vulnerable

As mentioned in Chapter 2, the CMM in which care is provided only to the economically vulnerable is

$$\max_{p,q} \pi = px(p,q) + r(\bar{x} - x(p,q)) - c(q\,|\,\bar{x}), \tag{2}$$

where Medicaid reimbursement r and bed supply $\bar{x}$ are given, and people choose private price p and quality of care q to maximize profits π.

To improve this model, first, reimbursement (r) needs to be associated with the current condition of each Medicaid care recipient. As stated earlier, r does not reflect user needs (see Chapter 2), and thus, it is important to categorize the Medicaid users into several grades, as Table 3.1[2] shows, and pay them r accordingly. Thus, Medicaid care recipients begin to consider price and quality of care at the very least as much as private care users do, and are not just given r:

$$\max_{p,q} \pi = px(p,q) + rx(p,q) - c(q\,|\,\bar{x}). \tag{2-1}$$

4.2.   Model using leverage

In the event that the results of the evaluation of care quality by public institutions are useable, there are cases in which it is possible to improve the quality of care by using leverage for evaluation items without incurring too much cost. For example, Kadoya (2011) used data on group homes in Japan, which are also used in Chapter 4, to investigate the causal relationships between the evaluation items. The results of this investigation clarified that showing and sharing the management philosophy for the long-term care facility to and with employees, and educating them about it, leads to improvement in the quality of care services. In other words, by showing, sharing, and providing education on the management philosophy, it is possible to improve care services by leveraging items for which relatively little costs are incurred for the improvements.

As explained in Chapter 2, in the conventional approach of setting the minimum level of care, as prices rise alongside improvements to quality, it has the side effects of lowering user satisfaction and preventing some users from accessing long-term care.

However, if the results of evaluations of care quality are useable, then by analyzing the improvement factors of these sorts of evaluation items, it becomes possible for the government to propose to the facilities methods of efficiently improving the evaluation of care quality. In other words, as shown in Figure 5.2, quality improves by moving the line for the amount of required care from $(y = qq^* + ii^*)$ to $(y = qq^{**} + ii^{**})$. Therefore, care is purchased at the intersection point (X^{**}) of the line $(y = qq^{**} + ii^{**})$ and the new indifference curve of the care recipients (U^*), with the quality of X^{**} being higher than that of X^*, and moreover, less expensive. In this way, the quality of care is improved without causing user dissatisfaction by raising prices.

Research in this field has only just begun, but if public information were used well, it would be possible to propose and provide consulting on highly cost-effective service-quality improvements. Yet, we need to note that the group home external evaluation result items are basically updated every three years. Therefore, it is necessary to be aware that the evaluation items shown in this book might already have been updated. Going forward, together with verifying

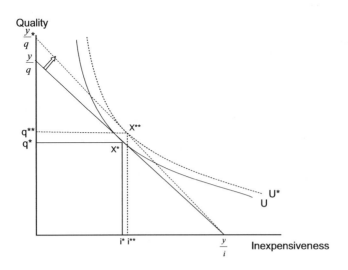

Figure 5.2 Care differentiation and equilibrium

the validity of the evaluation items, it is hoped that a method of improving service quality that uses the latest evaluation items and that does not incur costs will be investigated.

5.   Interim conclusion

The purpose of Part I was to answer the following research question: how should governments design the human service market in order to maintain a mechanism that ensures service quality? To answer this, this research adopted a model-testing approach, first presenting a CMM that directs market competition to enhance service quality. In the remaining part of Part I, this model is verified for the points of applicability, efficacy, and financial sustainability.

The purpose of the CMM is to provide an environment in which the long-term care recipients choose providers based on the quality of long-term care. To achieve this purpose, the CMM must satisfy four conditions: (a) the universal provision of long-term care services, (b) long-term care services standardized according to each of the conditions for the long-term care recipients, (c) restriction of price competition, and (d) public disclosure of quality information on the long-term care providers.

A flow chart of the CMM is depicted in Figure 5.3. First, as services are provided universally, all users are eligible to receive them by applying through the requisite long-term care test. Second, as the content of the care is standardized according to the conditions of the long-term care recipients, the government (or public institution) investigates the level of care required by users. Third, users select providers based on the categorization of care needs. As there is no price

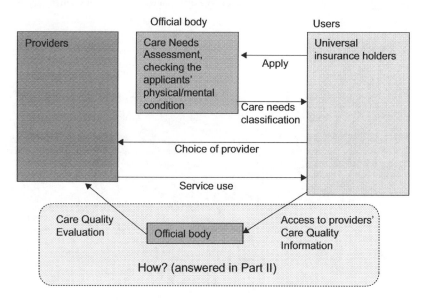

Figure 5.3 Flow chart of the CMM

competition in the market, users can choose providers based solely on the quality of their services. However, as there is information asymmetry in the human service market between users and providers, the government (or public institution) must publish information on providers' quality of long-term care.

This book proved that CMM is implementable. Surveying the long-term care markets in OECD nations, the research found that the Japanese LTCI market meets all four preconditions. Together with Japan, Austria, Germany, Luxemburg, Netherlands, Norway, Sweden, and South Korea meet the first condition of universal care. Furthermore, Germany, Luxemburg, and South Korea meet the second condition for standardized content of care according to care recipients' conditions. However, Japan is the only country that meets the third condition of restricted price competition.

This book supports the conclusion that the CMM is effective. Although the assumption that users have access to providers' care quality information contradicts information asymmetry models in the care market, this study proved that none of these conflicting models is fully supported. Moreover, this study found that when governments (or public bodies) publish providers' care-quality information, the more competitive the market becomes, the better the quality of the services that are provided. In addition, the findings added empirical implications to the literature of care-market information asymmetry models: (a) the contract failure model, (b) the MAR model, and (c) Suzuki and Satake's (2001) model.

Moreover, this book suggested that the CMM is financially sustainable. Analyzing the long-term care expenses of OECD nations, the research in this book revealed that the universal care system does not necessarily cost more than the means-tested system does. Investigating the merit good model and scale of economies, it was clarified that the cost efficiency of the universal care system is rooted in the small income gap of markets with the universal care system. This indicates that a small income gap is a precondition for the universal care system.

As a supplementary discussion to the CMM, this study proposed the use of the leverage model. In particular, this book presented a policy to improve quality, especially for markets that do not meet the precondition of a universal care system. This is a method of using leverage evaluation items in order to efficiently improve the evaluation of evaluation items. By incorporating advice and consulting, governments can efficiently enhance the quality of services.

This book proved that CMM is implementable, efficient, and sustainable. That is, CMM sustainably directs market competition to enhance the quality of services along with the care quality indicators approved by governments. The remaining question, as seen in Figure 5.3, is how to measure providers' care quality. The answer to this question is provided in Part II.

Notes

1 However, long-term care might not be as "rivalled" as a cake: care might be available to multiple customers.
2 The classification (i.e., the number of categories and their measurement) is not necessarily the same classification as Japan.

Part II

Performance measurement for the human service market

6   Outcome-based and process-based performance measurement model for the human service market

Analyzing the group home market in Japan, Part I demonstrated that the CMM directs market competition to enhance care quality. By setting appropriate performance indicators in the CMM, therefore, governments can logically solve the long-standing care quality issue, because performance measurement offers users guidance on choosing a provider.

The purpose of Part II is to investigate the best way to measure providers' performance in order to solve the long-term care quality issue. This chapter specifically compares outcome-based performance measurement and the alternative, process-based performance measurement.

1.   Clarifying performance measurement

The terms "performance measurement" and "performance indicator(s)" in this book are often referred to as care quality measurement and care quality indicator(s), respectively. Since this book defines providers' care quality as providers' performance, these terms are interchangeable in this book.

Why is it necessary to measure care quality? As discussed earlier, governments are required to assure the quality of human services because governments are responsible for providing people with a certain standard of living. Furthermore, most human service is provided through a competitive market in order to respond to increasing needs. Without performance measurement, it is difficult to ensure a level of standard care within this market. In addition, there tends to be information asymmetry between users and providers in human service markets. Without performance measurement, therefore, it is difficult for users to choose providers based on quality of services.

A key concept in performance measurement is viewpoint. Depending on the point of view, what to measure varies. For example, the manager of a care institution might measure profit from care services, whereas some users might measure the price of care services. Therefore, Behn (2003) presented a scheme to clarify "*how* should *who* hold *whom* accountable for *what*?"[1] As indicated in Table 6.1, *How* is identified with rewards and punishments. *Who* means the accountability holders, whereas *Whom* is the accountability holdees. Then, *What* is decided (i.e., the measurement).

Table 6.1 A way to answer the accountability question

Question	Accountability	Players
How?	With reward and punishment	Market competition
Who?	The accountability holders	Users/Governments
Whom?	The accountability holdees	Providers
What?	Standardized test scores	Performance measurement set by public authority

Source: Behn (2003)

The definition of the performance indicators in this book clarifies its point of view. Reward and punishment come from a competitive market mechanism. If a provider performs well, it attracts more users (i.e., reward) and vice versa (i.e., punishment). Accountability holders are users who need to know providers' care quality when choosing a provider and governments that manage the competitive market.[2] In other words, users and governments are the *who* in control of reward and punishment. Providers constitute the *whom* and should be held responsible for quality care provision. The performance indicators by which users and governments hold providers responsible are the *what*. Public institutions are in charge of performance evaluation.

2. Problem of outcome-based performance measurement in human services

The existing outcome-based performance measurement conflicts with the ambiguous policy goals of human service. In order for governments to implement outcome-based performance indicators, there need to be clearer goals. Along with goals, performance measurement provides information for decision-making for service users, especially when choosing a provider. Thus, market competition based on performance indicators directs providers to enhance service quality using the indicators that will lead to the achievement of the goals. "The clearer the goals and the better developed the performance measures, the more finely tuned the information for decision making can be" (Lipsky, 1980: 40). Providers become loyal to information for decision-making in the form of performance indicators. On the other hand, the less clear the goals are, the more poorly developed the indicators are; and the less accurate the feedback is, the more individuals in a service provision facility will be on their own (Lipsky, 1980: 40). In other words, non-government providers, particularly for-profit ones, aim to look after their own interests (i.e., profit maximization) rather than following information for decision-making of performance indicators. Nonetheless, the policy goals of human service are ambiguous. The provision of long-term care for elderly people, for example, commonly aims to ease aging-related ADL concerns and the degree of success in achieving such aims is very difficult to measure.

The reader might think that such an ambiguous goal can still be achieved. If the care addresses the elderly person's physical concerns, such as a knee problem, it would ease their concerns, meaning the achievement of the policy goal of long-term care. In addition, readers might believe that implementing customer satisfaction measures by questionnaires is a good idea to measure the outcome of care.

While evaluations based on customer satisfaction certainly have merit, these methods cannot solve the care quality issue, as they are applicable only to a group of care recipients. Many care recipients today suffer from unrecoverable conditions, such as dementia. In Japan, for example, the number of dementia patients has already increased to 4.62 million people, and this number exceeds 8.6 million people if including those with mild cognitive impairment (Asada, 2013). In addition, in the dementia prevalence rates by age group, it is estimated to be approximately 22 percent in the 80–84-year group and 41 percent in the 85–89-year group (Asada, 2013), while the number of dementia patients is expected to increase more and more alongside the aging of the population. Moreover, in most cases, care recipients with such cognitive problems are incapable of answering a questionnaire. The ambiguous policy goals of human service still get in the way of outcome-based performance measurement.

The ambiguity of the goals comes from human service's idealized dimension (Lipsky, 1980), which is evident in policy goals. For instance, Japanese LTCI aims "to go beyond simply the personal care of the elderly who need care, and to support their independence." Such goals, to help people be independent in their lives, are indeed "more like receding horizons than fixed targets" (Landau, 1973).

The origin of human service contributes to the abovementioned idealized dimension of goals, making the ambiguity of these goals inevitable. In other words, as discussed in Chapter 2, human service originates from the idea that governments ensure people a certain standard of living. In the case of long-term care, therefore, goals like easing aging-related ADL concerns certainly derive from the nature of human service.

3. Process-based performance measurement

Process-based performance measurement, used in traditional public institutions (see Table 1.8 in Chapter 1), suits the ambiguous policy goals of human service. Unlike outcome-based performance measurement, which focuses on *how much* is done, process-based performance measurement pays attention to *how* it is done. As process-based performance measurement does not look for the result but the process, this approach can accommodate the ambiguity of policy goals.

The measurement specifically assesses the behavior and training of frontline care workers (Lipsky, 1980[3]). For example, suppose we are assessing a nursing home's meal service by behavior. Instead of evaluating how much is achieved toward goals, the measure constructs the evaluation, assessing the process of meal service, including choice of utensils, customized cooking methods, taking meal requests, and recording nutritional needs. Such services are also assessed in terms of caregivers' skill-training backgrounds. Many types of ADL-related support do not seem to require experience and/or skills, but slight differences in experience and skills can make significant differences in the quality of care. For example, undressing frail care recipients is a simple but very delicate task and care of the elderly with cognitive impairments often requires communication techniques that are well above normal. These process indicators represent qualities that are hypothetically associated with good performance (Lipsky, 1980).

4.   Problem of process-based performance measurement

Process-based performance measurement has a significant weakness. The measurement requires very close communication between policymakers and frontline care workers, because the measurement of care workers' behavior and training is all about *know-how* of the service. Nonetheless, as mentioned in the Introduction, governments today do not have the *know-how* of service, as they no longer provide care directly. Indeed, the distance between governments and providers is one of the main reasons that outcome-based performance measurement is applied to the current governance scheme.

To make matters worse, another nature of human service makes the problem of process-based measurement even more serious. Unlike staff working on the front line in most organizations, care workers in the field of human service have a considerable amount of discretion in determining the nature, amount, and quality of benefits and sanctions provided by their agencies (Lipsky, 1980). The needs of human service are quite diverse and care workers need to customize their service for each user. For that reason, human service is very complicated and it is difficult to create manuals with general applicability. This makes process-based measurement even more difficult in the era of public administration services utilizing the market.

5.   Superiority of process-based measurement in human services

This chapter has reviewed the weaknesses of both outcome-based and process-based performance measurement in the field of human service. As seen in Table 6.2, both measurements have positive and negative aspects owing to the nature of human service.

Nonetheless, this book claims that, in the evaluation of human services, process-based measurement is superior to the existing outcome-based performance

Table 6.2 Strengths and weaknesses of the features of human service

	Outcome-based	*Process-based*
Ambiguous goals	–	+
Discretion of frontline workers	+	–

measurement. Whereas the weaknesses in process-based performance measurement can be compensated for, the downside of outcome-based performance measurement is crucial to the very quality of human life. For further discussion, this research first explains the most important considerations for performance measurement.

5.1. *Citizen needs as the most important factor*

Performance measurement focuses on reflecting citizen needs for evidence of the effectiveness of projects and policies (Wholey and Newcomer, 1997). As human service and all other public services are for the benefit of people, performance indicators need to coincide with people's needs. This value, in its purest form presently, is the basis of today's democratic societies. People's (or citizens') needs in human service are communicated from service users (care recipients).

Therefore, policymakers need to hear the voices of the current and potential service users to reflect their voices in services. In fact, most successful public services have designed, implemented, and revised care administration based on users' voices. The previously mentioned cases of telecommunication, delivery, and public transportation services are good examples.

Nonetheless, in the field of human service, this valuing of users' voices has served as an obstacle to service quality improvement. First, the demands of human service do not often come from the users themselves. In many cases, their family members are the source of the demands. Focusing on users' voices, the measurement tends to overlook this aspect of users' needs. Second, and more importantly, many users who need care the most are not capable of expressing their needs. Due to physical and cognitive constraints, a significant number of users cannot properly deliver their needs to policymakers. Moreover, unlike in the fields of telecommunications and public transportation, the quiet voice of these weaker members of society in human service does not mean they are unnecessary at all. The purpose of human service is rather to respond to such a quiet voice.

In human service, those who know the best about users' needs are frontline care workers. They are the only players who interact with both users and their families. Constantly interacting with users, only care workers can uncover hidden but very important care needs.

Performance measurement in human service must always include the voices of frontline care workers, because this is the only way to reflect users' needs in measurement. Thus, the weakness of process-based performance measurement is compensable. In human service, policymakers always need to interact with care providers.

5.2. *Outcome-based performance measurement as a crucial cause of low-quality care*

The weakness of outcome-based performance measurement is a crucial cause of the long-term care quality issue in the human service market. Human service, under this performance measurement, is likely to end up as the following two scenarios. First, government manages to set up a tangible policy goal to measure providers' performance, but any goal dissatisfies the users. As previously indicated, this is the nature of human service. In human service, a tangible (i.e., measurable) goal inevitably dissatisfies a group of users. For example, a resident's longevity might sound like a reasonable goal that can measure the performance of nursing homes. That is, the measurement assumes that the better care the nursing home provides, the longer the residents live. Nevertheless, achieving the goal does not necessarily satisfy the users. First, because of the measurement, many nursing homes will no longer accept users in poor health. In addition, users might suffer from unwanted care, which extends residents' life expectancies. In this case, regardless of the fact that long-term care is needed, those who lose access to nursing homes and residents who dislike life-lengthening care would feel unhappy about the goal along with the performance measurement.

Second, outcome-based performance measurement is inevitably inflexible. The measurement does not easily reflect updated behavior of the frontline care workers, because the relationship between governments and care providers is based on outsourced contracts. The users' needs are, on the other hand, continuously changing. For example, only a few decades ago, there was little demand for care for the elderly with dementia. Today, however, such care occupies a significant portion of long-term care needs. Changes in people's lifestyles, socioeconomic changes, and technological developments dramatically influence human care needs and responses to them. Those who know the best about these changes are frontline care providers, not bureaucrats in central government. It is precisely this frontline ideology that makes it possible for governments to adjust to changing needs.

The long-term care quality issue in human service has been partly caused by the use of outcome-based performance measurement, as both of the above scenarios indicate. The weakness of process-based measurement is compensable whereas the weakness of outcome-based measurement is crucial in terms of the care quality in human service. This book, therefore, argues that governments need to replace the existing outcome-based performance measurement with the alternative process-based performance measurement.

6.   The care policy model

In order to replace outcome-based performance measurement with process-based performance measurement, governments need to modify the current public policy model. The current model is designed to suit the use of outcome-based performance measurement, which does not require a close interaction between governments and providers. Such interactions are, on the other hand, necessary for the use of process-based performance measurement.

However, this modification does not aim to trigger a shift from the current public policy model to the traditional bureaucratic model. The author of this book agrees with human service provision through a competitive market, as Chapter 1 shows that such provision through the market is necessary to respond to increasing service needs. Moreover, Part I in this book justifies the utilization of the market in terms of the care market model.

The purpose of this section is to explain how governments and providers connect within the current governance of market utilization. This section specifically investigates how the interaction between governments and providers has been underestimated, analyzing a public policy model (a logic of governance) presented by Lynn *et al.* (2000) in the current governance model. Then, the research modifies the logic of governance in order to promote government–provider interaction, which is an important condition for the use of process-based performance measurement, and in addition presents the CPM.

6.1. Change of governance model

Since the 1970s, governments have become less hierarchical than previously, more decentralized, and increasingly willing to cede their role as the dominant policy actor to the private sector (Kettl, 2000). The last few decades have seen the rise of such governance and a reduction in the government's role as a direct supplier of public services. As a result, the role of governments has shifted to administration, making sure that market competition does not sacrifice service quality over cost, and working to ensure that market competition leads to improvements in the quality of public services.

These changes inevitably influenced a good deal of the existing public policy model. To keep up with the new reality, public administration scholars have been forced to re-conceptualize their theoretical foundations. For example, Peters and Pierre (1998) argued that four basic elements characterize discussion of governance: 1) dominance of networks, 2) the state's declining capacity for direct control, 3) blending of public and private resources, and 4) use of multiple instruments. According to their argument, governance is a body of models that comprehend lateral relations, inter-institutional relations, the decline of sovereignty, the diminishing importance of jurisdictional borders, and the fragmentation of the roles of public institutions. In addition, Kettl (2000) set out six core issues of new public management (NPM), a nominal designation of the new style of governance. The six core issues are 1) productivity, 2) marketization, 3) service orientation, 4) decentralization, 5) policy, and 6) accountability. NPM particularly characterizes the global public management reform movement that has redefined the relationship between government and society. This is, in fact, evident in nations associated with the Westminster model[4] (e.g., Australia, New Zealand, Canada, and the United Kingdom), in which NPM followed serious attempts to reform the public sector by defining and justifying what government should and should not do, and to reshape public service provision by criticizing the pathologies of bureaucracy (Kettl, 2000).

Nevertheless, among the most significant contributions to the literature of the current public policy model is the work of Heinrich and Lynn (2000) and Lynn *et al.* (1999, 2001). The authors, after compiling and analyzing the dispute on governance, presented the public policy model (a logic of governance) based on this governance theory.

6.2. The public policy model

As a result of the discussion, Lynn *et al.* (2000) present a public policy model (a logic of governance) to model the market-utilizing public policy model. From here, this book calls this logic simply the public policy model. As a step toward meeting the changing definition of governance, this model intends to establish a logic of governance to help support systematic research (Frederickson and Smith, 2003). In reduced form, Lynn *et al.* (2000: 15) presented their public policy model in the following compact form:

$$O = f[E, C, T, S, M]$$

O = Outputs/outcomes, which indicate the product of a governance regime.

E = Environmental factors, which can include political structures, level of authority, economic performance, the presence or absence of competition among suppliers, resource levels, and dependencies, legal frameworks, and the characteristics of a target population.

C = Client characteristics, which include the attributes, characteristics, and behavior of clients.

T = Treatments, which are the primary work or core processes of the organizations within the governance regime. They include organizational missions and objectives, recruitment and eligibility criteria, methods for determining eligibility, and program treatments or technologies.

S = Structures, which include organizational types, levels of coordination and integration among the organizations in the governance regime, relative degrees of centralized control, functional differentiation, administrative rules or incentives, budgetary allocation, contractual arrangements or relationships, and institutional culture and values.

M = Managerial roles and actions, which include leadership characteristics, staff–management relations, communications and methods of decision-making, professionalism/career concerns, and mechanisms for monitoring, control, and accountability.

Although the public policy model is useful for conceptualizing today's public policy model, it has faced some criticism. Ellwood (2000) claimed the model comes "close to the economist's criticism of political science: by including everything, one runs the danger of explaining nothing."

Nevertheless, these criticisms might turn out to be premature. Lynn *et al.* (2000) did not claim that the public policy model was a fully functional model; their goal was simply to theoretically and empirically address the governance of public policies and contribute to improving their criterion, implementation, and administration (see Lynn *et al.*, 2000). In fact, the public policy model, as a research program for a standard administrative theory, has already attracted the attention of scholars in the mainstream (Frederickson and Smith, 2003).

6.3. Theoretical challenge

The challenge of building a close relationship between governments and providers is illustrated in Figure 6.1, while the comparative traditional public policy model is shown in Figure 6.2. In the traditional model, public services are predominantly provided by governments, based on pressure from people through politicians. Thus, governments could easily measure the service process[5] for its own service provision.

In the current public policy model, on the other hand, public services are mainly provided by outsourced non-government sectors based on the treatment (i.e., performance measurement) set up by the governments. Thus, as Lynn *et al.* (2000) described, this model is O = f(E, C, T, S, M). The policy outcome depends on governance in that the government: 1) grasps the public needs by observing the social environment; 2) sets up the treatment (i.e., performance measurement) based on the client characteristics; 3) builds the structure of the market, outsourcing public service provision to non-government sectors; and finally, 4) manages the public service market.

The public policy model works well with outcome-based performance measurement, which is useful in many fields of public services. As mentioned earlier, such services as telecommunications, delivery, and public transportation, tend to have tangible goals and providers are usually expected to work precisely along

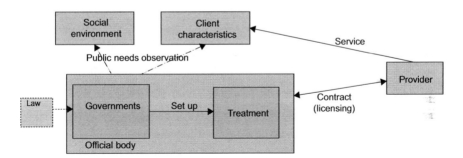

Figure 6.1 Current structure of Public Administration Model

Note: The dotted arrows indicate observation.

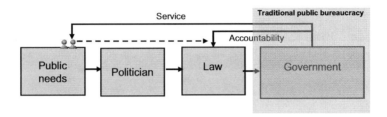

Figure 6.2 Traditional structure of Public Administration Model

the targets. Therefore, the outsourcing relationship between government and providers works effectively, even though they do not closely interact. Such tangible goals allow governments to measure the outcome-based performance of providers.

The public policy model is not suited for process-based performance measurement. This model tends to treat the relationship between public administration (i.e., governments in a broad sense) and providers as a contract-based, outsourcer–outsourcee relationship. In human service provision, however, it is very difficult to implement outcome-based performance measurement owing to the ambiguity of the policy goals and the considerable discretion of providers. On the one hand, the current public policy model has achieved decentralized policy networks, but on the other hand, the model is devoid of government–provider interaction.

Certainly, this does not mean that the current public policy model has completely overlooked the importance of the interaction between governments and providers. Lynn *et al.* (2000) recognize the need for interaction in their logic of governance. According to Lynn *et al.* (2000, 2001), any public governance regime is the outcome of a dynamic process that can be summarized by core logic. The process might be expressed in a set of hierarchical interactions in logic of governance (Figure 6.3). The concept of government–provider interactions is mentioned specifically in processes (d) and (e) in the logic.

Nonetheless, the public policy model does not satisfactorily highlight the importance of the interaction. As mentioned earlier, this would be fine for the provision of other public services, such as telecommunications, but it is not fine for the provision of human services. The model, thus, needs to be modified in order to fit the features of human service provisions.

Between (a) citizen preference and interests expressed politically and (b) public choice in enacted legislations or executive policies.

Between (b) public choice and (c) formal structures and processes of public agencies.

Between (c) the structures of formal authority and (d) discretionary organization, management, and administration.

Between (d) discretionary organization, management, and administration and (e) core technologies, primary work, and service transactions, overseen by public agencies.

Between (e) primary work and (f) consequences, outputs, outcomes, or results.

Between (f) consequences, outputs, outcomes, or results and (g) stakeholder assessments of agency or program performance; and, to close the circuit.

Between (g) stakeholder assessments and (a) public interests and preferences.

Figure 6.3 Hierarchical interaction in logic of governance
Source: Lynn *et al.* (2000, 2001)

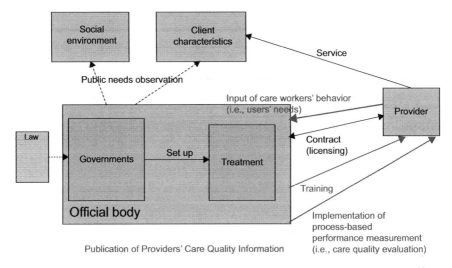

Figure 6.4 Care Policy Model

7. Modifying the public policy model

This research proposes the care policy model (CPM) to modify the public policy model so that it is suitable for the provision of human services. This CPM adds care workers' behavior (B) and the original model becomes O = f (E, C, B, T, S, M). Because receiving and acknowledging the input of provider's behavior is very important to access users' needs and to reflect the needs in performance measurement, this modification would solve the existing mismatch between performance measurement and users' needs.

The CPM is described in Figure 6.4. Besides the observation of the social environment and client characteristics, the government receives updated care workers' behavior.[6] Then, the government inevitably listens to the voices of frontline care workers. As a result, the treatment (i.e., performance measurement) truly reflects the users' needs.

8. Summary of chapter

Outcome-based performance measurement in the current public policy model was questioned in Chapter 1. This chapter compared outcome-based performance measurement and the alternative process-based performance measurement. Weaknesses were found in both measurements. Process-based performance measurement did not fit the current public policy model; and outcome-based performance measurement did not fit the ambiguous policy goals of human service. Favoring process-based performance measurement to solve the care quality issue, this research presented the CPM to fit the use of process-based performance measurement.

Process-based performance measurement under the CPM logically solves the care quality issue in the market, because the measurement reflects the users' needs and guides users to choose a provider based on its care quality.

Nevertheless, several empirical questions remain regarding the process-based performance measurement. Is it empirically applicable? Is it really possible to implement the process-based performance measurement model? Chapter 7 answers these questions, investigating a successful case in which the measurement reflects users' needs. This book specifically examines this case in comparison with another case, based on existing outcome-based performance measurement.

The second issue is about the training of care workers. The present chapter claimed that training improves the quality of care, but what kind of training is needed? In addition, it is assumed that training all care workers is very costly, especially when the number of care workers has been increasing in the era of an aging society. Is the required training financially sustainable? Chapter 8 answers questions regarding cost, explaining the impact on care quality improvement and national economies.

Notes

1 Behn (2003) presented two different ways of answering the accountability question, but this research only utilizes his simple "traditional way" to clarify the viewpoint.
2 In most types of human service provision, providers enter the market with licenses issued by governments (see Chapter 1 for details).
3 Lipsky (1980) described such frontline care workers as "street-level bureaucrats."
4 Another model, reinventing government, came much later and is unique to the United States, where there is less privatization, because local, state, and national governments in the United States share responsibility for most policy arenas and are subject to different political motivations. There is no central agent powerful enough to force functional re-organization on the scale pursued by the Westminster model (Frederickson and Smith, 2003).
5 This includes the behavior and training of service providers (i.e., street-level bureaucrats in this case).
6 Care workers' behavior indicates, for example, how care workers (i.e., providers) serve meals for care recipients. See Table 4.2 for details.

7 Investigating the empirical applicability of process-based performance measurement in human services provided through a competitive market

The purpose of this chapter is to consider the empirical validity of the presented process-based performance measurement model, in the human service market. To do so, this chapter specifically compares two typical cases: the Japanese long-term care market, which favors the presented process-based performance measurement, and the United States long-term care market, which focuses more on existing outcome-based performance measurement. Certainly, both process and outcome are sometimes interchangeable. For instance, skilling up of care workers is a process toward providing good quality of care, but such achievement could also be recognized as the outcome of a short-term goal toward providing good quality of care. In reality, there is no absolute process-based performance measurement or outcome-based performance measurement. Nonetheless, the cases of Japan and the United States, as later mentioned, clearly show their preferences (Table 7.1).

The bottom line is that care quality in the process-type Japanese market is less problematic than that in the outcome-type United States market. Wiener *et al.* (2007) compared quality assurance for long-term care internationally in selected OECD member nations and areas.[1] Using the extent to which care quality is perceived as a problem, Wiener *et al.* (2007) rated nursing homes in the United States as the most problematic, and those in Japan as the least problematic. Because the definition of long-term care varies by nations, this does not necessarily mean that care quality in Japan is superior to that in the United States. Nonetheless, the result indicates that Japan, with process-based performance measurement, responds better to perceived care needs.

Therefore, the following sections, after defining the providers in both countries, first analyze how outcome-based performance measurement fails to take users' needs into account in the United States, and how process-based performance measurement succeeds in reflecting them in the performance indicators in Japan.

Table 7.1 Models and cases

Case	Performance measurement	Public Administration Model
United States	Outcome-based	$O = f(E, C, T, S, M)$
Japan	Process-based	$O = f(E, C, \mathbf{B}, T, S, M)$

Note: O = policy outputs/outcomes; E = environmental factors; C = client characteristics; B = care workers' behavior; T = treatment (i.e., performance measurement); S = structure; M = management. See Chapter 6 for details.

Table 7.2 Care workers in the United States and Japan

	United States		Japan
Care workers	direct-care worker (DCW)	nursing aides, orderlies, and attendants	certified care workers (CCW)
		home health aides	early career care
		personal and home care aides	workers (ECCW)

1. Definitions of care worker in the United States and Japan

The definition of long-term care varies slightly by nation and so does the definition of providers (i.e., frontline care workers). Thus, first, we need to identify who provides care in both nations. As seen in Table 7.2, in the United States, a care worker is often called a direct-care worker. Furthermore, direct-care workers consists of three categories: (a) nursing aides, (b) home health aides, and (c) personal and home care aides. In Japan, on the other hand, the term "care worker" usually indicates a certified-care worker and a early career care worker. Certainly, assistant nurses in Japan often work for long-term care providers as well, but this chapter does not include them, because their main workplace is hospitals, not long-term care providers' facilities. For these reasons, "care worker" in this chapter indicates direct-care worker, certified care worker, and early career care worker; otherwise, direct-care worker is used only in the context of the United States and certified care worker and early career care worker in the context of Japan.

2. Outcome-based performance measurement in the United States

In the United States, almost every nursing home uses an indicator that expresses the physical and mental health of the care recipients. This evaluation indicator is called the minimum data set (MDS), and it is utilized by the government as a tool to measure the providers' performance in order to clarify ambiguous human service goals.

2.1. Background to outcome-based performance measurement

The MDS was originally developed to assess the conditional status of nursing home residents. Responding to the Omnibus Reconciliation Act of 1987, which was concerned about care quality issues in nursing homes, the Institute of Medicine (IOM) first designed the MDS to assess the functional, medical, mental, and psychosocial status of each resident (IOM, 1986). Licensed health-care professionals (usually registered nurses) who worked at the nursing home conducted the assessments.

The MDS committee recognized that the collected data could be used in a regulatory capacity (IOM, 1986). Surveyors could use the data to draw their resident samples and governments could use the outcome data to evaluate care providers' performance. That is, governments interpreted residents' functional, medical, mental, and psychosocial status as indicators of care quality.[2]

This was the turning point at which the United States began to apply outcome-based performance measurement. As in human service, the goal of long-term care in the United States contains ambiguity. The service is provided under the government aim of providing essential human services, especially for those who are least able to help themselves.[3] Due to the ambiguity of this goal for long-term care, the government had not previously measured the performance of providers. When poor care quality became a social issue, however, the government conducted actual condition surveys by investigating the physical and mental conditions of nursing home residents. Analyzing the results of resident assessments, the government began to examine the use of outcome-based performance measurement to evaluate nursing homes' care quality. In other words, the government translated the goal of essential human services into the care to maintain (or improve) users' physical and mental conditions.

Since then, the MDS has been used to develop publicly reported quality measures based on these conditional statuses of residents (Rahman and Applebaum, 2009). Table 7.3 indicates the development of MDS-based (i.e., outcome-based) performance measurement. In 1999, the Centers for Medicare and Medicaid Service (CMS) started requiring surveyors to use MDS-based measurement to guide their nursing home evaluations. In 2002, the CMS launched the Nursing Home Compare web site, a consumer information site that presents MDS-based quality ratings for virtually all nursing homes. Certainly, the MDS was initially criticized for its data collection. The data collection method was not well instructed, for example, and the time frame for assessment was based on a resident's admission, and then, on assessments undertaken every 90 days only, although major resident changes that occurred after the seven- or 14-day look-back period were supposed to trigger new assessments (Mehdizadeh and Applebaum, 2005). However, as the MDS has actively been revised, the instructions for data collection have been repeatedly updated and many nursing homes have gradually introduced assessment that is more frequent.

As a result, there have been undeniable improvements in resident outcomes (Rahman and Applebaum, 2009). According to Feng *et al.* (2006), for example,

Table 7.3 History of MDS

Year	Development
1990	MDS is introduced
1991	MDS is nationally implemented
1991	Enhanced MDS, MDS+, is developed for resource utilization group and quality indicator development project
1995	MDS 2.0 is nationally implemented
1995	Zimmerman *et al.* (1995) report on 24 MDS-based quality indicators
1998	Nursing homes are required to submit MDS data to CMS electronically
1999	State surveyors are required to use quality indicators to guide nursing home evaluations
2006	Nursing home Pay-for-Performance demonstration project is launched
2008	MDS 3.0 final draft is published
2010	MDS 3.0 is implemented nationally

Source: Rahman and Applebaum (2009)

the pressure ulcer incidence of residents clearly dropped, despite increases in residents' acuity, and restraint use decreased for those provided with care. With regard to the extent to which the use of the MDS, or the MDS-based performance measurement, contributed to care quality improvement, a series of studies, reported in 1997, evaluated the effect of MDS use on selected resident outcomes (Fries *et al.*, 1997; Hawes *et al.*, 1997; Phillips *et al.*, 1997). On the whole, the researchers found improvement in outcome measures from pre- to post-MDS implementation.

Nonetheless, nursing home care quality in the United States has been perceived as problematic. Wiener *et al.* (2007) compared quality assurance for long-term care in the United States, England (the United Kingdom), Australia, Germany, and Japan. The authors rated the nursing homes in the United States, together with England, as problematic in the category of the extent to which (care) quality is perceived as a problem. Due to the absence of a common measurement, this did not necessarily mean that the care quality of the United States' nursing homes was among the worst. However, to be perceived as problematic by the public is a serious matter in the provision of human service, which aims to ensure people's minimum standard of living.

2.2.   *Outcome-based performance measurement as a cause of users' dissatisfaction*

The problem with public perceptions of care is not due to a lack of effort to develop a quality assurance system. As mentioned in Chapter 2, in fact, only the United States and Japan have introduced nationwide providers' care quality evaluation systems, which target all providers in the long-term care market, with the United States having a longer history of developing a viable system than Japan.

The problem in the case of the United States is a result of its theoretical base: the outcome-based performance measurement with the public policy model. Faced with requirements for tangible goals, which are necessary for outcome-oriented performance measurement, the government simplified the original ambiguous goals of long-term care by translating the physical and mental conditions of residents into enhanced, measurable outcomes.

Certainly, the health conditions of residents might have occupied a significant component of the original goals, initially. Nevertheless, as mentioned in the previous chapter, human service needs continuous change. Although most users wanted to improve their conditional status when the performance measurement was implemented, such desire has gradually decreased (or it has become an assumption of basic care) and residents and their families have begun to look for other conditions, programs, and environments promoting quality of life. Today, in fact, many elderly people suffer from incurable conditions, such as dementia. Those who suffer from such conditions find no value in the outcome-based performance measurement, because the condition is not curable. It is natural for these residents to prefer other factors, such as peaceful environments and relaxed atmospheres, to the MDS-based rehabilitation.

Furthermore, many researchers have questioned the MDS's value as a performance measurement tool, citing problems with its dearth of residents' quality-of-life indicators (Bates-Jensen *et al.*, 2003; Ouslander, 1997; Rahman and Applebaum, 2009; Schnelle, 1997; Schnelle *et al.*, 2003; Simmons *et al.*, 2003; Uman, 1997). However, there is no tangible definition of quality of life. Conducting a research survey, Slevin *et al.* (1998) revealed that the correlation between medical doctors' and patients' definitions of quality of life was very poor. Outcome-oriented approaches cannot be implemented in the field of human services that deals with quality of life.

Indeed, this is what the previous chapter mentioned: the weakness of outcome-based performance measurement in the human service market. The measurement creates gaps between the measurements and users' needs, and the gaps cause users to be dissatisfied. In the case of long-term care in the United States, as health concerns and trends change, many users value their quality of life over the improvement of their physical and mental conditions. Outcome-based performance measurement has not accommodated the changes, because the measurement systematically lacks input from care workers. As a result, the voices of users who do not intend to (or cannot) improve their conditions is overlooked and many who suffer from incurable conditions lose access to long-term care. This is because the more improvement that can be shown in the users' conditions, the better the assessment of the nursing home and the better the services the nursing home is perceived to provide in the context of outcome-based performance measurement.

3. Process-based performance measurement in Japan

The care quality in Japan's long-term care market is perceived as least problematic (Wiener *et al.*, 2007). The process-based performance measurement in the Japanese market is based on the CPM, which adds care workers' behavior into the existing model: O = f (E, C, B, T, S, M). Like all other human service markets, the Japanese long-term care market has ambiguous goals. The strength of process-based performance measurement is, however, the measurement that can accommodate the ambiguous goals as they are.

3.1.   Background of introducing process-based performance measurement

Process-based performance measurement in Japan originates from the idea that society should adjust to the convenience of frail elderly. In fact, the Japanese government embarked on a process of restricting the social security system in conjunction with the rise of long-term care demand, including ascertaining the objective of long-term care when providing it in a form for the elderly separate from health insurance.[4] Although responding to long-term care needs is commonly a social security issue in OECD nations, the emphasis is, indeed, slightly different from the case of the United States, which has perceived elderly-related issues as dangers of or to an individual's independent life as well as challenges arising from the physical constraints of aging.

A major reason for Japan's attitude that society should be changed toward the elderly is the rapid increase of its long-term care needs. In fact, unlike the United States and many other OECD nations, the proportion of elderly in Japan's population suddenly increased from around 1990 (Figure 7.1). Furthermore, according to the MHLW (2002), about 13 percent of the elderly aged

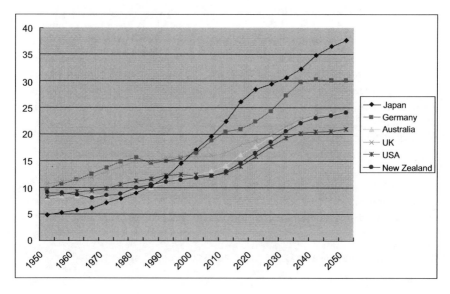

Figure 7.1 Percentage of population aged 65 years and above (Unit: 10,000 people)
Source: United Nations (2008)

65 years or above in 2000 needed long-term care[5] and the proportion is expected to reach 16 percent[6] in 2025.

Japan's approach to the long-term care issue comes from long-term care service being a substitute for family caregiving. Since the preparatory period of the LTCI policy, in approximately 1987, the government has actively surveyed the demography of insufficient family caregivers[7] and planned policy to address this lack. These surveys included the condition of care recipients (Table 7.4), demography of bedridden elderly (Figure 7.2) and future estimation (Figure 7.3), caregivers for bedridden elderly (Figure 7.4, 7.5), and female labor participation ratios (Figure 7.6). In addition, the training for the licensing of certified care workers began prior to 1987.

In summary, Japan considers long-term care service as a role to be shared between society and care recipients' families. Therefore, in this sense, it is inevitable that the focus is placed on who is responsible for the care, or in other words, how the care is provided (the process) rather than on the care outcome.

Table 7.4 Conditions of care recipients

Category	1993	2000	2010	2025
Physically weak elderly people	100	130	190	260
Suffering from dementia and in need of long-term care (except for the bedridden elderly)	10	20	30	40
Bedridden elderly (including elderly who are bedridden and suffering from dementia)	90	120	170	230
Total (elderly needing long-term care, etc.)	200	280	390	520
Population of elderly people (aged 65 years or over)	1,690	2,170	2,770	3,240

Source: MHLW (2002)

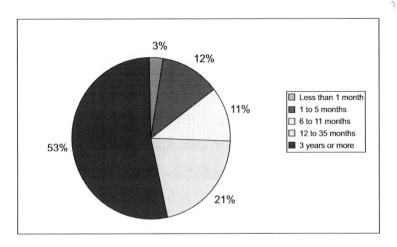

Figure 7.2 Percentage of bedridden people by bedridden periods

Source: MHLW[8] (1995)

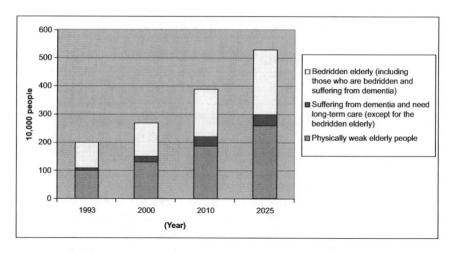

Figure 7.3 Future estimation of the bedridden elderly/elderly people suffering from dementia

Source: MHLW (2002)

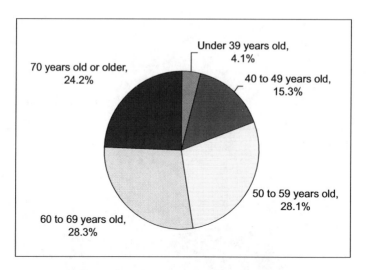

Figure 7.4 Caregivers for the bedridden elderly (age group)

*Main caregivers who live with bedridden people aged 65 years or over: 244,000 people

Source: MHLW (1995)

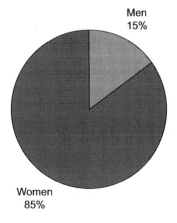

Figure 7.5 Caregivers for the bedridden elderly (male vs. female)
Source: MHLW (1995)

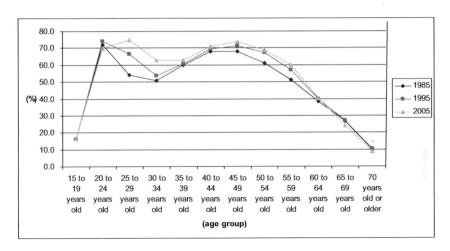

Figure 7.6 Female labor participation ratio in Japan
Source: Ministry of General Affairs (2006)

3.2 *Process-based performance measurement as a guide for care implementation*

Process-based performance measurement reflects care workers' behavior in the measurement. In Japan, there are three types of quality information about providers available in the market, as shown in Table 3.6 in Chapter 3, and all of them evaluate how care is implemented, not how successful the care is. For example, instead of asking about the conditions of the care recipients before and after the care, each information type asks about the system for providing the care. The focus is placed on the extent to which the collaboration between the health, medical, and welfare services has been achieved, and it is asked whether the provider has a database of provided services. In addition, as shown in Table 4.2 in Chapter 4, the indicators describe the details of the care process (i.e., choice of utensils, arrangement of meals, and atmosphere of dining) for the evaluation items for meal provision. These detailed process measurements are serving as a guide for care implementation for the providers.

4.   The CPM: promoting interaction between governments and providers

As mentioned in Chapter 6, process-based performance measurement requires close interaction between governments and providers in order to reflect users' needs in the measurement of care workers' behavior. While the existing public policy model does not possess that function because of its outsourcer–outsourcee relationship, the CPM systematically includes the interaction between the government and providers. This section investigates how the Japanese market applies the CPM in the system, using a comparison with the United States market with the existing model.

The Japanese long-term care market implements the CPM by giving care workers career path opportunities to be involved in the process of policymaking and implementation. Table 7.5 indicates care workers' career advantages compared with those of the United States. In Japan, the work experience of care workers serves as a gateway to higher positions of care eligibility judgment, care planning, performance indicator setting, and the implementation of measurement, whereas no such system exists in the United States.

4.1.   *Judging users' eligibility grade*

In Japan, a prefectural Care Level Assessment Committee, which includes care workers as members, assesses users' eligibility grades. The committee membership must include specialists in the field of healthcare, medicine, and welfare (Article 14–15, LTCI Act; Article 9, LTCI Government Order). Municipalities assign them two-year terms based on advice from local professional associations, such as medical associations. In most cases, a medical doctor[9] represents the field of medicine; a public health nurse represents the field of healthcare; and a certified care worker (or certified care manager) represents the field of welfare. Each assessment requires a computer-based eligibility test and further assessment from five randomly chosen committee members with at least one from each field. Table 7.6 indicates the job titles of Care Level Assessment Committee members in Kakogawa city, Hyogo, which is a typical mid-sized city in Japan. The total number of committee

Table 7.5 Summary of care workers' career path advantages in policymaking positions

Setting and implementation of performance measurement		Japan	United States
Judging users' eligibility grade	Care worker's involvement/precedence	✓	*(no eligibility grades exist)*
	Remarks	Certified Care worker is to be a member of the care level assessment committee	*(no eligibility grades exist)*
Creating care plan	Care worker's involvement/precedence	✓	-
	Remarks	Care plan is created by a certified care manager whose eligibility requires 5 years' work experience as a certified care worker	Certified nurse, medical doctor
Setting performance indicators (i.e., Japan: third-party evaluation; US: minimum data set)	Care worker's involvement/precedence	✓	-
	Remarks	Government's Performance Indicator Setting Committee*, which includes several activists with care worker experience as well as representatives of care providers	MDS committee of IOM
Implementing performance measurement	Care worker's involvement/precedence	✓	-
	Remarks	Certified evaluator (those who have experience as care workers are eligible to skip some part of the training)	Usually licensed healthcare professionals (e.g., certified nurse), employed by the nursing home (CMS, 2010).

* Kaigo saabisu no shitu no hyouka ni kansuru chosa kenkyuu iinnkai.

members varies by the size of the municipality: a more populated municipality has a bigger number and vice versa.

In the United States, on the other hand, there is no system of eligibility grade, although the assessment of MDS might be very close to it. However, it is predominantly certified nurses, not care workers, who assess the MDS.

Table 7.6 Job titles of CLAC members: the example of Kakogawa city

Municipality (population)	Medicine	Healthcare	Welfare	Total members
Kakogawa city (about 268,830)	Medical doctor: 24 Dentist: 2 Pharmacist: 2	Nurse: 13 Occupational therapist: 1 Physical therapist: 1 Dental hygienist: 1	Certified care worker: 6 Certified social worker: 2 Mental health welfare professional: 1 Social welfare officer: 1	58

Source: Hakit21 (2010)

Note: All job titles require official certificates. Nurse indicates both certified nurse and assistant nurse.

4.2. Creating the care plan

Only a certified care manager can suggest a care plan for each user. Although care workers cannot directly carry out the process of making a care plan, the work experience of care workers is, nevertheless, advantageous to becoming a certified care manager (Figure 7.7). To take the national examination to become a certified care manager, applicants are required to have work experience with care-related licenses. Together with other care-related professionals, such as medical doctors and nurses, care workers (i.e., certified care workers and early career care workers) are entitled to take the national examination with five years' work experience.

There is no such system in the United States. As the outcome-based performance measurement is aimed at improving users' conditional (i.e., physical and mental) status, care plans are usually suggested by medical professionals.

Therefore, the CPM implemented in Japan systematically incorporates the voices of care workers into the care plan. Those who make care plans for users inevitably have care worker experience; new officers keep coming up from the front line with current experience and understanding of the changing long-term care market. This allows the care plan to reflect updated care needs.

4.3. Setting performance indicators

While medical professionals at the Institute of Medicine (IOM) create the MDS in the United States, Japanese third-party evaluation is developed by frontline care workers. Table 7.7 indicates the job titles of the Japanese performance indicator-setting committee at the Ministry of Health, Labour and Welfare,

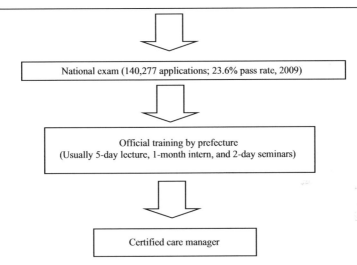

Eligibility

a) 5 years' working experience in one of the following national-licensed care-related fields:
   1) medical doctor, 2) dentist, 3) pharmacist, 4) public health nurse,
         5) accoucheuse, 6) nurse, 7) assistant nurse, 8) physical therapist,
         9) occupational therapist, 10) social welfare counselor,
         11) certified care worker, 12) orthoptist, 13) prosthetist,
         14) dental hygienist, 15) speech therapist, 16) japanese traditional massager,
         17) acupuncture/moxacautery expert (*hari kyu shi*),
         18) judo-orthopedics expert

b) 5 years' working experience as a consultant at a designated care-related facility (e.g., handicapped care and long-term care)

c) 5 years' working experience as one of the following licensed care-related workers.
   1) certified case workers (*shakaifukushi shuji*)
   2) early career care workers (formerly known as trained heme helper [2nd grade])

d) 10 years' working experience as a non-licensed care assistant in a related position at a designated care facility

National exam (140,277 applications; 23.6% pass rate, 2009)

Official training by prefecture
(Usually 5-day lecture, 1-month intern, and 2-day seminars)

Certified care manager

Figure 7.7 How to become a certified care manager

Source: Tokyo Metropolitan Foundation for Social Welfare and Public Health (2017)

Note: "Official training by prefecture" is the case of Tokyo metropolitan area. The content of the official training might vary slightly by prefecture.

Japan. The committees includes 11 of 17 job titles from long-term care providers and their professional organizations, or seven of 13 members from long-term care providers and their professional organizations. Moreover, 45 providers and certified evaluators contribute to the model survey of the performance indicators. It is natural that the third-party evaluation in Japan reflects the voice of frontline care workers.

Table 7.7 Job titles of performance indicator-setting committee

Committee member

Summary

6 from professional organizations

5 from long-term care providers

2 from research institutes

1 from medical provider (hospital)

1 from local government

2 from public utility organizations

Total: 17 (13 members)

*Some members were from more than one type of organization

- Vice president of public utility organization, Japan Group Home for the Elderly with Dementia Association (*kouekishadan houjin nihon ninchishou group home kyoukai*), president of a health service facility for the elderly
- Chief facilitator of All Japan Group Home network
- Member of public utility organization for dementia elderly and family in Chiba prefecture
- Administrator of group home for elderly with dementia
- Executive director of public utility organization, Japan Group Home for the Elderly with Dementia Association (*kouekishadan houjin nihon ninchishou group home kyoukai*), president of special nursing homes for the elderly
- <u>President of Hospital</u>
- Courier of All Japan Group Home network, president of Nagano prefecture's Group Home Association
- Member of public utility organization for dementia elderly and family in Chiba prefecture
- Chief researcher of Dementia Care Information Network
- Member of welfare research institute
- Chief of Social Welfare Department, Fukuoka prefecture
- President of Health Service Facilities for the elderly
- President of Okayama prefecture's Day Service Association, president of All Japan Group Home Network, Okayama prefecture

Note: The underlined designation indicates the committee chair.

Model survey participant

45 community-based service providers (36 group home providers, 9 community-based providers of one-stop home-care service for small groups of users)
14 members of performance measurement committee

Source: MHLW (2006c)

4.4.   *Implementing performance measurement*

In Japan, certified evaluators, many of whom have experience being care workers on the front line, conduct external quality evaluations. As Figure 7.8 shows, experience as a care worker is one step to becoming a certified evaluator. Since the external evaluation has a strong focus on care workers' behavior, it is

Application eligibility
- 1 year's working experience as a certified care manager
- 3 years' care-related working experience in the fields of medicine, healthcare, and welfare (or equivalent, e.g., trainer/lecturer experience in a related field).
- Not belong to any long-term care provider

Prefectural training

Certified evaluator*

*The certificate is valid for 5 years, after which evaluators need to participate in prefectural training to renew their certificates.

Figure 7.8 How to be an evaluator
Source: MHLW (2008a)

reasonable for local governments to provide care workers with ways to become certified evaluators. As a result, the implementation of performance measurement reflects the care workers' views.

5. Positive effect of process-based performance measurement with the CPM

Having many policymakers who have experience as care workers, governments can reflect detailed care needs in long-term care policy. Table 7.8 shows all services within the Japanese LTCI scheme. A wide range of programs is available, from rehabilitation to dementia care, from day care to night care, from care prevention to sanatorium-type medical care, and even home rehabilitation for elderly people living at home as a choice.

Combining the diverse services, users can receive long-term care that meets their needs. Figure 7.9 shows a sample service combination, for a case in which the user decides to stay home and not live in a facility service (i.e., nursing home). A local government[10] suggested the example. To receive such services,[11] other than in the case of the high-income group, 10 percent of the fees are paid privately by the recipient and 90 percent are covered by the universal insurance. The users can choose multiple home-visit services, including (medical) nursing care, rehabilitation, home care (ADL support), and counselling. They can also use commuting services, such as day service (or day care) to socialize with other elderly people and not just to receive comprehensive ADL support or rehabilitation. If the users become bedridden, they can expect to receive visiting services three to four times a day, plus

Table 7.8 Choice of care services (detailed)

At-home care	Institutional care
Home-visit services	**Community-based services**
• Home-help service • Home-visit nursing • Home-visit bathing service • Home-visit rehabilitation • Management and guidance for in-home care	• Group home for the elderly with dementia
	Support to prevent the need for care
Commuting services	**Community-based services**
• Day-care service • Day rehabilitation service	• Community-based one-stop home care service for small group of users • Day care service for the elderly with dementia
Short-stay services	**Community-based prevention programs**
• Short-stay for the elderly requiring care • Short-stay for the elderly requiring medical care • Residential care facility for the elderly requiring care • Rental service for welfare equipment • Sales of designated welfare equipment	• Projects to prevent the need for care • Comprehensive support projects • General counselling support projects • Rights advocacy projects • Comprehensive and continuous care management support projects • Care management projects to prevent the need for care • Optional projects
Community-based services	**Facility Services**
• Community-based one-stop home care service for small groups of users • Night care service	• Health services facilities for the elderly • Special nursing homes for the elderly • Sanatorium-type medical care facilities
Others	
• House reform	

Source: MHLW (2008a)

night service as necessary. Nevertheless, the users can expect to receive even more comprehensive, long-term care when they choose to stay at facility services, because care workers do not need to commute for caregiving, as in at-home care. Such a wide range of long-term care services can be said to indicate how the care workers' voices (i.e., users' needs) are reflected in the policies of Japan's system, applying the process-based performance measurement with the CPM.

Support 1

	Mon	Tue	Wed	Thu	Fri	Sat	Sun
AM	Day Service or Day Care			Home help			
PM							

Support 2

	Mon	Tue	Wed	Thu	Fri	Sat	Sun
AM	Home help	Day Service or Day Care			Day Service or Day Care		
PM				Home help			

Care 1

	Mon	Tue	Wed	Thu	Fri	Sat	Sun
AM	Home help	Day Service or Day Care	Home help	Visiting Nurse	Day Service or Day Care	Home help	
PM							

Care 2

	Mon	Tue	Wed	Thu	Fri	Sat	Sun
AM	Day Service or Day Care	Home help	Day Service or Day Care	Visiting Nurse	Day Service or Day Care	Home help	
PM				Home help			

Assisted device (renting): Wheelchair

Figure 7.9 A standard weekly at-home care plan (Support 1–Care 5)
Source: Niigata city (2014)

Care 3

	Mon	Tue	Wed	Thu	Fri	Sat	Sun
AM	Day Service or Day Care	Home help	Day Service or Day Care	Visiting Nurse	Day Service or Day Care	Home help	
PM	Home help	Home help	Home help	Home help	Home help	Home help	Home help

Assisted device (renting): Wheelchair, special bed, and mattress

Care 4

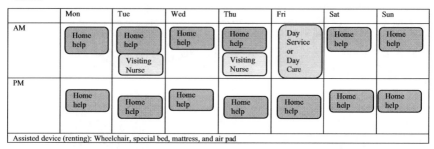

Assisted device (renting): Wheelchair, special bed, mattress, and air pad

Care 5

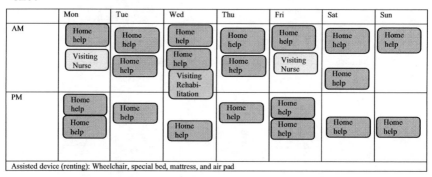

Assisted device (renting): Wheelchair, special bed, mattress, and air pad

Figure 7.9 (Continued)

6. The virtuous circle of the process-based performance measurement model

The positive effect of process-based measurement with the CPM is not just the excellent response to care needs, but also the sustainability of such a situation. Tables 7.9 and 7.10 indicate the outcome of the top three concerns in nursing home care and at-home care policies, from a survey of 12 selected OECD nations' public officers. Among the concerns, the recruiting of skilled care workers is the most common issue. A common challenge in long-term care provision, then, is to recruit and train capable and skillful care workers. The career path to be a policymaker, offered by process-based measurement with the CPM, is a factor attracting such care workers in Japan.

Care workers tend to be considered low-paid, simple laborers with very few career prospects in most countries, despite their increasing importance and responsibility in society. In the United States, for example, direct-care workers (i.e., care workers in the United States) earn near-poverty wages. As Figure 7.10 shows, the wage of direct-care workers is below that of other simple laborers. More than 41 percent of direct-care workers' households rely on some kind of public benefit, such as the Supplemental Nutritional Assistance Program (SNAP, also known as the "food stamps" program) (PHI, 2009). The ratio of care workers who do not have health coverage is nearly double that of other occupations (Figure 7.11). Ironically, those who provide care have much less access to healthcare than others. As caregiving is considered simple labor, there are few systematic career advantages, and thus, it has become extremely difficult to attract excellent human resources. On the other hand, the demand for advanced care skills is steadily increasing as care needs become more diverse (e.g., dementia care).

Of course, the treatment of care workers in Japan has much room to improve. According to a survey of the Japanese Association of Certified Care

Table 7.9 Policy concerns about the quality of nursing home care

Group of issues mentioned	*Countries*
Recruiting and retaining an adequately educated and skilled workforce; improved qualification of staff	**12 countries that replied to this question**
Implementation or further development of a quality assessment and monitoring system	Austria, South Korea, United States
Co-ordination of care service	Canada, Hungary, Germany
Building quality and amenity	Hungary, Japan
Other supply constraints: downward pressure on fees/inadequate fees paid to providers; lack of enough time for staff	New Zealand, United Kingdom, Korea (shortage of government subsidies)
Access to broader range of services, more differentiation	Norway, Austria (number of short-stay units)
Other mentioning of "top concerns" (country specific)	Use of physical restraints (Japan); Number of liability claims; lack of liability insurance for long-term care (United States)

Source: OECD (2005: 69)

Notes: Data are based on replies from national administrators to the following question: "What are the top three concerns in your country in terms of quality of institutional care?"

Table 7.10 Policy concerns about the quality of at-home services

Group of issues mentioned	*Countries*
Recruiting and retaining an adequately educated and skilled workforce; improved qualification of staff	**Majority of countries that replied to this question**
Improvement of skills of care managers	Canada, Japan
Implementation or further development of a quality assessment and monitoring system; improved standards framework	Australia, Austria, South Korea
Co-ordination of care services; continuum of care	Australia, New Zealand
Lack of information about services	Japan, United Kingdom
Prevention of inappropriate residential care admission	Australia
Supply constraints; limited financing	Korea, United States
Broader range of services; too little differentiation	Canada, Norway, United Kingdom
Adequate care supply for dementia cases	Germany, Japan

Source: OECD (2005: 70)

Notes: Data are based on replies from national administrations to the following question: "What are the top three concerns in your country in terms of quality of home care?"

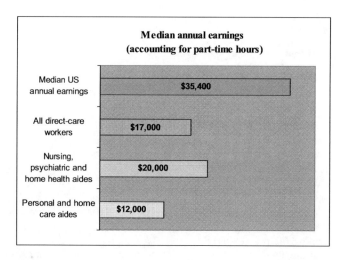

Figure 7.10 Direct-care workers' low wages

Source: Paraprofessional Healthcare Institute (2010)

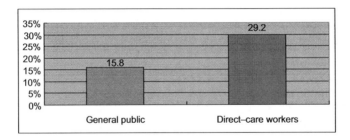

Figure 7.11 Direct-care workers lacking health coverage (%)
Source: Paraprofessional Healthcare Institute (2008)

Workers (2005), 47.8 percent of certified care workers identify low wages as occupational dissatisfaction from multiple answers. As a result, the turnover rate of care workers (21.6 percent) is higher than the combined average of all other industries (15.4 percent) (Care Work Foundation, 2008). Moreover, from fiscal 2015, LTCI remuneration has been reduced, and wages are forecast to fall even more.

However, the performance measurement with CPM in Japan helps to solve this problem, with the care workers' career path advantages toward being policymakers. Although caregiving might begin with simple labor, it can lead to higher positions with higher wages. This certainly might be a factor attracting a capable workforce in Japan.

Moreover, a progressive system applies to Japanese care workers' wages. First, the government guides the wages of care workers. The system takes working experience and acquired skills into account. Although the guidance is very detailed and complicated, as a result, as Table 7.11 shows, the progressivity of salary reflects actual work conditions. Second, the wage significantly increases as the care worker acquires a higher level of license. If, for example, a certified care worker, which is among the lowest levels of certified care positions, acquires a certified care manager's license, his or her salary increases sharply. On the other hand, compared to the survey of the MHLW, in which 47.8 percent of certified care workers identify their low wages as occupational dissatisfaction, the ratio drops to 36.3 percent for certified care managers.

The care workers' job market in Japan attracts a capable labor force as a direct result of process-based measurement with the CPM. Certainly, the low wage remains as a concern of care workers. However, the attractive career paths available, leading to policymaking positions, and the progressive salary system reasonably benefit existing care workers and attract new workers who are interested in healthcare-related careers.

Table 7.11 Actual condition survey of certified care workers' salaries (yearly) in Japan

Column: education; row: experience	Compulsory education only	High-school graduate	2-year junior college graduate	University graduate	Total
Less than 1 year	N.D.	N.D.	N.D.	JPY 3,498,120 (USD 34,981)	JPY 3,498,120 (USD 34,981)
1 year	N.D.	N.D.	N.D.	JPY 3,445,886 (USD 34,4589)	JPY 3,445,886 (USD 34,459)
2–3 years	N.D.	N.D.	N.D.	JPY 3,422,434 (USD 34,224)	JPY 3,422,434 (USD 34,224)
3–4 years	N.D.	JPY 3,524,360 (USD 35,244)	JPY 3,598,701 (USD 35,987)	JPY 3,759,356 (USD 37,594)	JPY 3,719,525 (USD 37,195)
5–6 years	N.D.	N.D.	JPY 3,867,120 (USD 38,671)	JPY 3,985,331 (USD 39,853)	JPY 3,979,421 (USD 39,794)
7–9 years	N.D.	JPY 3,927,800 (USD 39,278)	JPY 3,871,712 (USD 38,717)	JPY 4,352,265 (USD 43,523)	JPY 4,175,495 (USD 41,755)
10–14 years	N.D.	JPY 4,086,404 (USD 40,864)	JPY 5,040,950 (USD 50,410)	JPY 5,097,907 (USD 50,979)	JPY 4,869,521 (USD 48,695)
15–19 years	N.D.	JPY 4,249,240 (USD 42,492)	JPY 5,217,939 (USD 52,179)	JPY 6,341,404 (USD 63,414)	JPY 6,217,255 (USD 62,173)
20–24 years	N.D.	JPY 5,633,941 (USD 56,339)	JPY 6,034,183 (ADU 60,342)	JPY 6,917,815 (USD, 69,178)	JPY 6,656,289 (USD 66,563)
25–29 years	N.D.	JPY 5,307,040 (USD 53,070)	JPY 6,982,284 (ADU 69,823)	JPY 7,237,960 (USD 72,380)	JPY 6,906,164 (USD 69,062)
30–34 years	JPY5,220,120 (USD 65,252)	JPY 5,753,727 (USD 57,537)	JPY 7,364,764 (USD 73,648)	JPY 7,591,954 (USD 75,920)	JPY 7,177,755 (USD 71,778)
35 years or above	N.D.	JPY 7,463,673 (USD 74,637)	JPY 8,051,006 (USD 80,510)	JPY 7,529,076 (USD 75,291)	JPY 7,643,208 (USD 76,432)
Total	JPY5,220,120 (USD 65,252)	JPY 4,904,065 (USD 49,041)	JPY 5,455,358 (USD 54,554)	JPY 5,579,403 (USD 55,794)	JPY 5,490,568 (USD 54,906)

Source: Survey by the Japanese Association of Certified Care Workers (2005) with 3,549 answers out of 12,000 questionnaire (by mail) distributed in February 2005
Notes: Salaries are *after tax*. Due to the universal care and pension system in Japan, health insurance and pension are paid *separately* by the employer. N.D. indicates no data.

7. Summary

Analyzing the two empirical cases, this chapter proved that the long-term care market responds better to users' needs when governments implement the process-based performance measurement model. Investigating the case of Japan, the research showed that process-based performance measurement reflects users' needs (i.e., garnered from care workers' behavior toward and understanding of the high needs of users). In addition, the CPM supports governments' comprehension of citizens' demands via their direct inclusion of and interactions with care workers.

The case of the United States endorsed the weakness of outcome-based performance measurement. Cutting off the ambiguity of the policy goals, outcome-based performance measurement failed to reflect users' needs. The existing public policy model did not closely connect the governments and providers (i.e., care workers) and, as a result, the gap between users' expectations and provided service expands, resulting in user dissatisfaction.

The next chapter investigates another aspect of process-based performance measurement: care worker training.

Notes

1 The research compares England, which is a part of the United Kingdom, together with the United States, Germany, Japan, and Australia.
2 This outcome-based performance measurement is heavily influenced by Donabedian (1987)'s model, which used the concept of structure, process, and outcome. In the model, outcome is assumed to result from process, and process is assumed to require structure. In the model, therefore, a good outcome justifies the process and then the structure.
3 Department of Health and Human Services, The United States <www.hhs.gov/about/>
4 See the MHLW (2002).
5 The elderly people who needed care in 2000 (2,800,000 people)/elderly population in 2000 (21,700,000) = 12.9%.
6 The elderly people who needed care in 2025 (5,200,000 people)/elderly population in 2000 (32,400,000) = 16%.
7 The survey, titled *Comprehensive Survey of Living Conditions of the People on Health and Welfare,* is well known and has been revised every three years since 1987.
8 This ministry changed its name from the Ministry of Health and Welfare, Japan to the Ministry of Health, Labour and Welfare, Japan in 2001.
9 A medical doctor also serves as the chair of assessment in most cases.
10 The source is the handbook in Niigata city (2014), a local city in the northwest of Japan.
11 This might not be the case in a remote area.

8 Care workers' training

As the previous chapter investigates the behavior of care workers, this chapter examines another aspect of process-based performance measurement: care workers' training. There are two purposes. The first is to investigate what kind of training is needed for care workers to pick up users' needs. The second is to verify whether training is sustainable in the current situation, in which the number of required care workers has been increasing.

1.   Overview of care workers' training

Policymakers in many nations have realized that the improvement of care workers' skills and qualifications is significant to ensuring quality of care. As mentioned earlier in Tables 7.9 and 7.10 (Chapter 7), public officials commonly raise insufficient training for care workers as a policy concern.

However, in reality, the importance of care workers' training has been seriously overlooked in most countries. In fact, only the United States and Japan have introduced a common, minimum training system for care workers on a nationwide level. All other countries have yet to define fully who care workers are, because care institutions in these countries can in fact hire anyone to provide long-term care.[1]

In the United States[2] and Japan, on the other hand, common training is required to be a care worker. Compare the situation to driving a car. That is, one does not need a driver's license to drive a car on private property, but a license is required to drive on public roads, otherwise doing so is illegal. Likewise, everyone in the United States and Japan can provide long-term care to family members, friends, and others casually. Without required training, however, long-term care cannot be provided through public channels, which are Medicaid long-term care facilities in the United States[3] and the universal LTCI scheme in Japan. It is illegal otherwise to conduct care behavior.

The United States and Japan have very different approaches toward care workers' training. The training in the United States is concise and focuses on exercising proper care and protecting care workers from their potential job risks, including injury. In Japan, on the other hand, the training is comprehensive and focuses on understanding care recipients in order to pick up their detailed care needs. In order to investigate the effectiveness of care workers' training, therefore, this chapter continues to compare the cases of the United States and Japan.

2. Definition of care worker

Table 8.1 reviews the definition of care workers in the United States and Japan. Although they have different names, their tasks are similar. They mainly give ADL support to care recipients at care facilities (i.e., nursing homes) and in recipients' homes.

The roles of nursing aides and assistant nurses are, however, slightly different due to the difference of long-term care systems in the two nations. In the

Table 8.1 Definition of care workers in the United States and Japan

United States (direct-care workers)	Japan (care workers)
Nursing aides generally work in nursing homes, although some work in assisted living facilities, other community-based settings, or hospitals. They support residents' adl, such as eating, dressing, bathing, and toileting. In addition, they perform clinical tasks, such as range-of-motion exercises and blood pressure readings.	**Assistant nurses** generally work in hospitals, although some work in institutional care (i.e., nursing homes). They support patients' (residents') adl, such as eating, dressing, bathing, and toileting. They also perform clinical tasks, such as range-of-motion exercises and blood pressure readings.
Home health aides provide essentially the same care and service as nursing assistants, but they assist people in their homes or in community settings under the supervision of nurses or therapists. They might also perform light housekeeping tasks, such as preparing food or changing linen.	**Certified care workers** "provide appropriate advice and coordination as well as personal care to cope with physical and/or mental situations of those who need help in daily life, based on professional knowledge and skills" (certified social workers and certified care workers law of 1987).
Personal and home care aides* work in either private or group homes. In addition to providing assistance with adl, these aides often help with housekeeping chores, meal preparation, and medication management. They also help individuals go to work and remain engaged in their communities. Consumers directly employ and supervise a growing number of these workers.	**Early career care workers (*kaigo shokuin shoninsha kensyu*, formally known as trained home-helpers)** "are registered under the exclusive qualification name of eccw**" (enforcement order article 3–1(2), long-term care insurance law). The tasks include (a) "care services," such as assistance eating, bathing, clothing, and moving; (b) assisted housekeeping, such as cooking, laundry, cleaning, and shopping; (c) mental care for care recipients and their families; and (d) care advice for care recipients' family members.

Source: Bureau of Labor Statistics (2010)

Note: ADL indicates Activities of Daily Living.

* Personal and home care aides have many titles, including personal care attendant, home care worker, personal assistant, and direct support professional (the latter work with people with intellectual and development disabilities).
** Although ECCW is a prefectural license, the required qualifications (training) are designated by the Ministry of Health, Labour and Welfare.

United States, nursing aides, home health aides, and personal home care aides are called direct-care workers. They all work mainly in long-term care industries. In Japan, on the other hand, in fact nursing assistants mainly work at hospitals, not in long-term care industries, though certified care workers and early career care workers mainly work at long-term care industries.

The difference is rooted in the definition of long-term care in these countries. As Figure 8.1 shows, the care system is uniquely in charge of public long-term care in the United States. In Japan, on the other hand, long-term care exists across three different schemes. Whereas the universal LTCI scheme covers elderly-related conditions only, medical-related long-term care and disabled-related long-term care are covered by the public universal healthcare scheme (i.e., hospitals) and the public disability insurance (i.e., disabled care facilities), respectively.

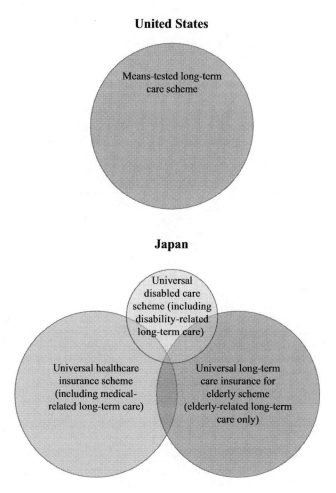

Figure 8.1 Differences in long-term care schemes in the United States and Japan

3. Extremely long training hours in Japan

The number of hours required to be a care worker in Japan is much higher than in the United States. Table 8.2 summarizes the required training hours in the two nations. The required training hours for a certified assistant nurse and certified care worker in Japan are 1,890 and 1,800[4] hours, respectively, whereas that of their counterparts in the United States is only 75. The difference is about 24 times. The mandatory training for early career care worker to apply for certified care worker in Japan amounts to 450 hours (130 for early career care worker qualifications), whereas that of the United States counterpart amounts to 75 hours. This time, the difference is not as significant, but Japanese training hours are still greater than are those in the United States.

Certainly, in the United States, many state governments add extra hours of training to the federal minimum requirement. In fact, 27 states and Washington, DC, require extra hours of training. Among them, in 12 states and Washington, DC, the training hours increase to 120 hours in total. In Japan, on the other hand, the training hours usually do not differ by prefecture, although assistant nurse and early career care workers are prefectural licenses (Certified Care Worker is a national license).

Nonetheless, there is an enormous difference in the number of required training hours between the United States and Japan. Moreover, in Japan, in order to respond to diversifying care needs, including dementia care, the training hours of certified care workers increased in 2009 from 1,500 to 1,800 hours. Early career care workers are now encouraged to complete a total of 450 hours of training. Furthermore, the licenses of trained home-helpers, together with certified assistant nurses, are criticized for having few required training hours. According to MHLW (2008b), many policymakers have proposed abolishing both licenses, in which case, current license holders would be required to upgrade to certified nurses[5] and certified care workers, respectively. In the United States, on the other hand, the minimum requirements have not changed

Table 8.2 Required training hours in Japan and the United States

	Japan	*United States*
Position	certified assistant nurses (CAN), certified care workers (CCW), early career care workers (ECCW)	direct-care workers (DCW)
Required hours of training	CAN: 1,890 hours CCW: 1,800 hours ECCW: 130 hours	75 hours (including 16 hours clinical training)

Source: Welfare and Medical Service Agency (2010b), Bureau of Labour Statistics (2010) and Welfare and Medical Service Agency (2015)

for a while, although some researchers have proposed increasing the training hours (e.g., Li and Ziemba, 2009).

4.   Two phases of training content

The purpose of care worker training is to acquire the necessary skills and forms of behavior toward care recipients to provide good quality of care. There are approximately two phases to achieving success. The first phase focuses on the safe conduct of requested physical support. This is fundamentally the focus of training in the United States. Moreover, the second phase focuses on picking up potential care needs and responding to them. This is necessary, especially when providing care for the elderly with dementia. The Japanese training is at this stage.

4.1.   Phase 1: case of the United States

To be able to respond to visible care needs, the first phase of training focuses on basic attitudes and physical skills. The attitudes trained here involve basic legal/ethics matters, human rights, and communication. They are somewhat considered as the basic skills in the profession. The skills trained are specific, and they include basic medical-related skills and transfer techniques. Since almost all care recipients are elderly, the basic medical-related skills are always necessary in case of emergency, though care workers are responsible only for first aid and not for medical treatment. As for transfer techniques, the training in Phase 1 includes not only giving smooth support, but also protecting care workers' own health. Throughout the ADL support, care workers often need to lift care recipients, as physically, care recipients are much more delicate yet often heavier than, say, the materials at a construction site. In fact, direct-care workers have the highest rate of workplace injuries among occupations in the United States (Zontek *et al.*, 2009). Back injuries, especially, are very common.[6] The training in Phase 1, therefore, covers forms of behavior and skills for visible care. Table 8.3 indicates the content of the training in the United States. Concerning nursing aides, resident rights correspond to the forms of behavior, whereas such aspects as clinical training, basic nursing, personal care, and basic restorative care are about skills. As for the case of home health aides/personal and home care aides, information regarding personal hygiene corresponds to behavior. The indicators of these skills are safe transfer techniques, reading and recording vital signs, infection control, and basic nutrition.

4.2.   Phase 2: case of Japan

Aimed at picking up potential care needs, Phase 2 emphasizes the mental and communication aspects in the training. As a significant number of care recipients suffer from cognitive impairments, many care needs are invisible. Elderly people might require help to go to the bathroom, assistance changing their

Table 8.3 Training content in the United States

Title	Content	Hours
Nursing aides	Clinical training	16
	Other skills	59
	• Basic nursing	
	• Personal care	
	• Mental health and social service	
	• Care of cognitively impaired	
	• Basic restorative	
	• Resident rights	
	Total	**75**
Home health aides/ Personal and Home Care Aides	Covered area:	75
	• Information regarding personal hygiene	
	• Safe transfer techniques	
	• Reading and recording vital signs	
	• Infection control	
	• Basic nutrition	
	(+ 16 hours practical training*)	
	Total	**75**

Source: Bureau of Labour Statistics (2010)

Note: * is required in many states.

position in bed, or support changing their clothes. However, if they cannot properly convey their intention, due to their cognitive conditions, such needs are easily overlooked. In order for care workers to pick up these potential needs, they must understand care recipients' attitudes and communicate effectively with them.

Communication does not just help care recipients, but also protects care workers' health. Care work is, indeed, a very mentally draining task, because care recipients' mental status tends to be unstable. As most care recipients are living the last stages of their lives, they inevitably face a fear of death while in care. According to Kübler-Ross (1969), there are usually five stages of grief as a pattern of adjustment to human death. These are denial, anger, bargaining, depression, and acceptance. This means that, at each stage, care recipients can be very emotional and care workers must face and deal with these dramatic reactions while giving care. A survey of Kawamura (2008) reported[7] that about 28 percent of care workers receive "physical and verbal abuse from care recipients"; this is a significant work concern. In such an environment, it is very important for both care recipients and care workers that care workers are capable of dealing with such emotions by communicating with care recipients effectively.

The focus of the Japanese training has shifted to this Phase 2. Tables 8.4 to 8.6 show the required training content for assistant nurses, certified care workers, and early career care workers. As in the training of assistant nurses, the mental aspect of care recipients is covered by several subjects, such as the psychology of the patient, psychiatric nursing, and practical psychiatric nursing, and a total of 175 hours are spent on these issues. Moreover, in order to understand care recipients further, the practical subjects have special focus on recipient groups, such as adult/elderly and mother/child. A total of 595 hours of training are spent specifically on adult and elderly care in order to understand their particular

Table 8.4 Required training for assistant nurses in Japan

Subject		Type	Hours
Basic	Language arts	Lecture	35
	Foreign language	Lecture	35
	Other general education	Lecture	35
Basic special	Human body function and structure	Lecture	105
	Diet and nutrition	Lecture	35
	Medicine and nursing	Lecture	35
	Illness	Lecture	70
	Infection and prevention	Lecture	35
	Care and ethics	Lecture	35
	Psychology of patient	Lecture	35
	Structure of healthcare and social welfare/nursing and law	Lecture	35
Special	Basic nursing		
	General consideration of nursing	Lecture	35
	Basic nursing skills	Lecture	210
	General consideration of nurse practice	Lecture	70
	Nursing for adult/nursing for elderly	Lecture	210
	Nursing for mother and child	Lecture	70
	Psychiatric nursing	Lecture	70
	Nursing practice		
	Basic nursing	Practice	210
	Nursing for adult/nursing for elderly	Practice	385
	Nursing for mother and child	Practice	70
	Psychiatric nursing	Practice	70
Total			1,890

Source: Welfare and Medical Service Agency (2010b)

Table 8.5 Required training for certified care workers

Subject			Hour
Human and society	Understanding humans	Human dignity and independence	30
		Human relationship and communication	30
	Understanding society	Understanding society	60
	Selective subjects	1. Life science studies	120
		2. Mathematics and logical thinking on human relations and social life	
		3. Basic life skills (e.g., life culture and living skills)	
		4. Leadership and human relations	
		5. Social studies (sociology, political science, and economics)	
		6. Various social welfare schemes	
Care	Basic care		180
	Communication skills		60
	Life support skills		300
	Care process		150
	Comprehensive care workshop		120
	Care practice		450
Mental and physical	Understanding dementia		60
	Understanding disabilities		60
	Mental and physical structure		120

Source: Welfare and Medical Service Agency (2010b)

needs and issues. In the training of certified care workers, these aspects are more clearly emphasized (Table 8.5). Besides practical training, many subjects deal with understanding human mentality. Topics include human dignity and independence, human relationships and communication, understanding society, leadership and human relations, social studies, communication skills, understanding dementia, understanding disabilities, and mental and physical structures. Indeed, 460 hours, about 26 percent of the total training, are spent on such matters.[8] Comparing this to the previous version of training content, the difference is clear. This trend is the same for home-visit care workers (Table 8.6). In summary, the focus of the Japanese training is on understanding and communicating with care recipients. This is how care workers in Japan are trained to identify potential care needs.

Table 8.6 Required training for early career care workers

Subject	Hours
Understanding duties	6
Dignity of care workers/self-support	9
Basics of care	6
Understanding care and social welfare services/collaboration with medical services	9
Communication skills on care work	6
Understanding aging	6
Understanding dementia	6
Understanding disabilities	3
Physical and mental structure and support skills	75
Reflections	4

Source: Welfare and Medical Service Agency (2015)

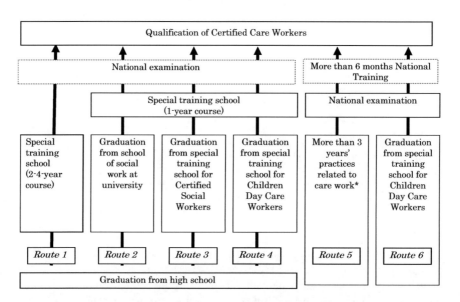

Figure 8.2 Six routes to qualify as a certified care worker
Source: MHLW (2010a)
* "Practices related to care work" means on-the-job training through the non-licensed part of nursing home tasks, such as cleaning rooms and cooking meals for care recipients.

5.   License examination

Whereas the completion of the training usually means qualification for the license in the United States, the completion of training in Japan might indicate only the qualification for a license examination. First, Japanese assistant nurse candidates (i.e., those who complete the required training at designated institutions) need to pass a prefectural examination to obtain a license.

Table 8.7 Subjects of certified care worker exam

Written examination
• Compendium of Social Welfare
• Elderly Care
• Disabled Care
• Rehabilitation
• Social Welfare and Care Support Skills
• Organizing Recreational Activities
• Psychology of Elderly and Disabled People
• Domestic Science
• Medicine
• Mental Health
• Compendium of Care Work
• Care Skills
• Care Skills on Various Occasions
Practical Examination (corresponds to the written examination, especially the subject of "Social Welfare and Care Support Skills")

Source: MHLW (2010a)

Table 8.8 Examination pass rate of certified care workers (2006–2010)

Year	*Examinees*	*Successful examinees*	*Success ratio*
2010	153,811	77,251	50.2%
2009	130,830	67,993	52.0%
2008	142,765	73,302	51.3%
2007	145,946	73,606	50.4%
2006	130,034	60,910	46.8%

Source: MHLW (2010b)

As for certified care workers, the examination is implemented universally.[9] As Figure 8.2 shows, there are now six routes to be a certified care worker and the examination will be implemented in all routes. In addition, the examination is not merely a formality. There is a wide range of subjects (Table 8.7) and only around 60 percent of candidates pass the examination every year, as shown in Table 8.8.[10]

6. Attracting excellent human resources

The purpose of this chapter was to investigate care workers' training as a part of the process-based performance measurement that ensures quality of care. Analyzing the cases of the United States and Japan has provided theoretical evidence that the care workers' training has two phases and that both are useful to ensure quality of care. Whereas Phase 1 standardizes the care quality of overt needs by ensuring proper care behavior and physical skills (e.g., transfer techniques), Phase 2 enables care workers to respond to potential care needs by teaching care recipients' attitude and training communication skills to pick up potential care recipients' needs.

Nonetheless, a concern is whether this type of training can attract talented human resources. As seen in the case of Japan, while on the one hand, the population of care recipients is expected to increase, on the other hand, the content of training has become more comprehensive. Can Japan continue to secure talented human resources for the next decade of an aging society?

A part of the question was already answered in the previous chapter. Compared to many other countries, in Japan there are incentives to choose a career as a care worker. In other words, experience as a care worker is becoming a necessary step to participate in policymaking in the field of care. For example, even currently, in order to take the examination to be a certified care worker, the qualification that brings together the tasks of preparing a care plan for care recipients and coordination as a long-term care service provider, it is necessary to have more than five years of practical experience as a long-term care welfare worker.[11] In addition, if the candidate has workplace experience as a care worker, there is a measure in which they are permitted to sit the examination for difficult qualifications too, such as the social worker qualification, even without a specialist degree. In other words, a path to advance their careers is opened up to care workers through their workplace experience.

Moreover, the government currently envisions a mechanism to make this career path more comprehensive. While retaining the existing career path, as shown in Figure 8.3, while care workers accumulate experience in their careers, they improve their skills to be certified care workers and specialist care workers, and finally, career paths open up to them in which they can utilize their experience and knowledge from the field, for example, as experts in a specialist field, such as dealing with dementia; an expert in long-term care education; or an expert in management and administration in the field of long-term care.

From these measures, the government in Japan, for both the quality and quantity of care, is providing overwhelming support for the training of care workers and the process evaluation system, and is implementing the CPM. By indicating a clear career path to care workers who are required to undergo the significant burden of long-term training, the number of registered care workers is in fact steadily increasing (Figure 8.4). This is in contrast to other countries, which, although recognizing the importance of training care workers, are unable to implement it due to worker shortages. For example, the United States relies on immigrants for 21 percent of its care workers[12] (PHI, 2009), while this percentage in Japan is less than 1 percent.[13] Of course, there are many issues facing Japan in its LTCI market, which are summarized in Chapter 10. However, at the very least, from the verification of the case of Japan, it has been proven that the CMM presented in Chapter 7 is fully functioning in this country in terms of securing the minimum level of care quality.

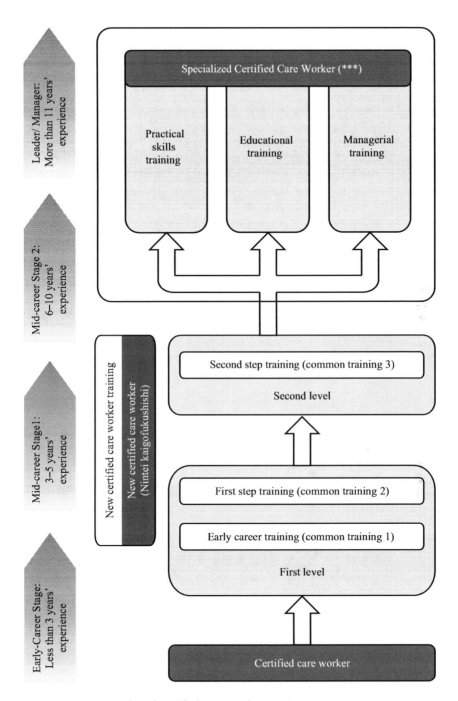

Figure 8.3 Career paths of certified care workers in Japan

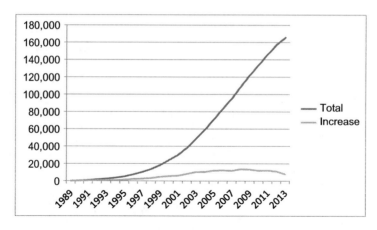

Figure 8.4 Number of registered certified care workers
Source: MHLW (2014)

Notes

1 "Care worker" mentioned here does not include medical staff, such as medical doctors and nurses. Certainly, in many countries in the West, in a lot of cases, nurses play an important role in care (Hotta, 2012). However, this is attributable to classifying some part of post-surgical nursing care as care in those countries. In this book, such nursing is excluding from the classification of care in order to focus on care for the elderly.
2 Some states do not require any training for the category of personal and home care aides.
3 In the United States, all long-term care facilities, including for-profit and non-profit ownership, are required to register with local governments (state governments in most cases). Therefore, "public channels" here do not mean public institutions only.
4 With regard to certified-care workers, the required training can be replaced by three years of on-the-job training at certified care facilities. In that case, however, candidates have to pass the national examination in order to ascertain that the candidate has completed the equivalent of the required training.
5 A certified nurse requires 3,000 hours of training and must take a national examination.
6 In Japan, about 70 percent of care workers suffer from back pain (MHLW, 2008b).
7 The survey was conducted in Japan, but the concern is considered shared in the United States and other countries, because the core workers' tasks are quite similar.
8 As for the selective subjects, each training hour is calculated by the total hours divided by the number of subjects (i.e., $x = 120/6$).
9 Until 2012, the exam was only for candidates in routes 5 and 6 (Figure 8.2).
10 The exam is an absolute evaluation, not a comparative assessment.

11 However, people can take the entrance exam if they have a statutory qualification and five years or more practical work experience other than as a certified care worker, such as a doctor, dentist, pharmacist, nurse, or physiotherapist, or if they have five or more years of practical experience in consulting assistance work. However, about half of those who pass the exam are certified care workers.

12 The PHI defines immigrants as those born outside of the United States,

13 Certainly, in the national care workers' examination in 2014, based on the EPA, there were 78 foreign nationals who passed the examination, which was 7.8 percent of the total number of people who passed in that year. However, based on the EPA, the cumulative number of foreign nationals who have passed the examination is still only about 100 people, and it estimated that practically all of those taking the examination not based on the EPA are Japanese nationals born in Japan. Therefore, they constitute no more than approximately 0.1 percent of the total number of 998,484 people (MHLW, 2015) who have passed the exam.

9 An industrial policy to ensure the sustainability of the care market model

As seen in the previous chapter, the motivation of care workers in Japan is relatively high. That said, in the context of the rapid aging of the Japanese population, it is costly for the government to train candidates to be care workers and to maintain the long-term care system.

However, as explained in Chapter 8, the training of care workers in Japan incorporates a mechanism to pick up the potential care needs of the elderly receiving long-term care. The task of picking up these potential needs can be referred to as "market research" in the terminology of economics and business, and can be converted into an industrial policy to respond to population aging. While on the one hand, training care workers incurs costs and creating a mechanism to provide the best possible care meets potential needs, on the other hand, converting the needs acquired thereby into an industrial policy and ensuring the sustainability of a long-term care system, at the very least, can be considered not unrealistic objectives.

As described in the Introduction, long-term care to meet the needs of the elderly will increase for the time being. According to estimates of the Budget Bureau, the Ministry of Finance (2014) (Figure 9.1), the total amount of spending on LTCI, which was 3.3 trillion yen in 2000, had increased to 8.4 trillion yen by 2012, and will reach approximately 20 trillion yen in 2025. As normally 10 percent of LTCI is paid for by the recipient (20 percent in the case of high-income earners), the market is expected to reach a scale in excess of 20 trillion yen when combined with the part paid privately by users. Moreover, as mentioned in the Introduction, population aging is occurring not only in Japan, but also in many other countries, and an increase in long-term care costs is expected accordingly. Therefore, at the very least, the market is forecast to expand rapidly worldwide over the next decade.

Moreover, long-term care is currently an extremely labor intensive field, with considerable room for productivity improvement as an industry. The movement of the elderly, support for their daily activities, including meals, washing, and using the toilet, and other life support, is carried out by care workers with some exceptions, and this has hardly changed at all over the last decades. In other words, there is considerable room for productivity growth in long-term care services. Here, if an industry is created in accordance with care needs, such as

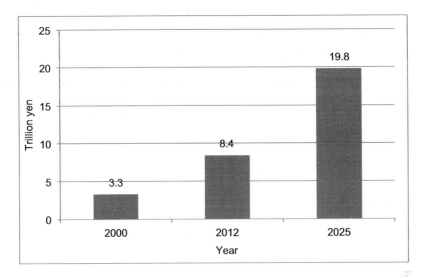

Figure 9.1 Estimated spending on LTCI

for welfare equipment and life-support robots that heighten productivity, economic growth would be possible (i.e., increased tax revenue), which would supplement spending on public long-term care. For example, in the current situation, for bathing assistance, there are tasks that require several care workers for one long-term care recipient. However, if these tasks could be carried out by only one long-term care worker through introducing mobility robots and cranes, the productivity of long-term care services would improve (i.e., the quantity of long-term care services provided by one long-term care worker would increase), thereby creating demand for mobility robots and cranes. In addition, understanding the health status of each individual long-term care recipient, such as their blood pressure and body temperature, up until now has taken several hours, but this could be completed in a few minutes using health monitoring systems. This would improve the productivity of long-term care and promote the industries of the relevant systems. Under the economic principles of capitalism, wealth is concentrated in producers who are most productive (Mankiw, 2014). Fundamentally, long-term care entails supporting the actions of long-term care recipients in their daily lives, and so by widening our horizons, it is evident there is room for these productivity improvements hiding in the shadows of practically all actions.

Of course, when referring to long-term care, some users would likely feel a sense of resistance to the idea of improving the productivity of "human service," which has been carried out manually by people for many years, through industrialization in the form of welfare equipment and robots. Certainly, long-term care using equipment and robots would seem to possess a weak point in that they lack warmth compared to long-term care carried out by people.

However, it is highly possible that not many long-term care recipients are seeking this warmth. Figure 9.2 shows the results of a survey by the Ministry of Health, Labour and Welfare conducted among 4,465 men and women nationwide, showing the percentages of the wants of the person in question and their families in the event that the person needs long-term care. The majority of the family respondents wanted the person to receive long-term care at their own home from their family or a combination of family and external services, but less than 30 percent of the long-term care recipient respondents themselves wanted this. In terms of other answers also, many of the long-term care recipients themselves selected such answers as moving to a paid-for nursing home or luxury assisted-living homes, from which we understand that more than their families realize, they want to be "independent" and not rely on their families. The same results are evident in the "Questionnaire on Living Preferences and Levels of Satisfaction, 2013 Edition" conducted by Osaka University. This questionnaire was sent to randomly selected men and women aged 20–69 years nationwide, and answers were received from approximately 4,300 people.[1] The results showed that the actual situation is that parents, more than their children imagine, do not want "long-term care by children," even though this would seem to offer more warmth (Table 9.1).

As a result, it would seem that the spread of welfare equipment and related robots that increase productivity would take place without much resistance. If the productivity of long-term care services improves, it would become possible

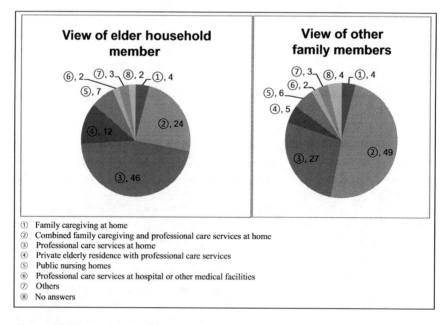

Figure 9.2 View of desired long-term care

Source: MHLW (2010c)

Table 9.1 Views about long-term care

	Completely disagree				Completely agree	Mean	Observations
Child(ren) should take care of their parents when they require long-term care	1	2	3	4	5	3.59	4,327
If I had a child (children), I would want my child (children) to take care of me when I require long-term care	1	2	3	4	5	3.15	4,327

Note: The order of the scale was converted from the original in order for readers to comprehend the results easily.

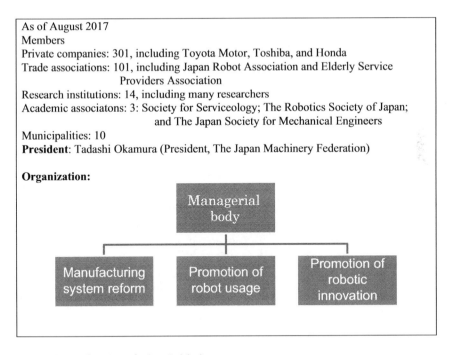

As of August 2017
Members
Private companies: 301, including Toyota Motor, Toshiba, and Honda
Trade associations: 101, including Japan Robot Association and Elderly Service
　　　　　　　　　Providers Association
Research institutions: 14, including many researchers
Academic associatons: 3: Society for Serviceology; The Robotics Society of Japan;
　　　　　　　　　and The Japan Society for Mechanical Engineers
Municipalities: 10
President: Tadashi Okamura (President, The Japan Machinery Federation)

Organization:

Managerial body

Manufacturing system reform | Promotion of robot usage | Promotion of robotic innovation

Figure 9.3 Robot Revolution Initiative
Source: Robot Revolution Initiative (2017)

to accept more long-term care recipients using fewer workers. In addition, it is conceivable that the advance of the automation of mobility would advance the independence of the elderly who conventionally would have had to rely on assistance. In addition, the industrial promotion of welfare equipment and robots can be expected to greatly stimulate the economy and lead to an increase in tax revenue, which is the source of funds to maintain and develop the LTCI system. To repeat this important point, promoting this industry would greatly assist the abilities of care workers to draw out potential care needs. A virtuous circle is created, in which providing the elderly with the best care improves the sustainability of the public long-term care system.

1.　Long-term care as a source of economic growth

The Japanese government, especially the Ministry of Economy, Trade and Industry (METI), depicts a growth strategy utilizing the skills of care workers, of the ability to draw out potential care needs. Specifically, the Japanese government is focusing on promoting welfare equipment and life-support robots in collaboration with care workers. Life-support robots assist with long-term care services, housework, and people's safety and security in their everyday lives (AIST, 2007). This initiative began with the "21st Century Robot Challenge Program," announced by the METI in 2001, the year after the enforcement of LTCI. Since then, the experience of care workers who received full training is being greatly utilized for the research and development of life-support robots. First, robot manufacturers, robot users (care workers and long-term care recipients), universities, local governments, think tanks, insurance companies, venture companies, and leasing companies gathered and established a joint organization called the Robot Revolution Initiative (formally known as the Robot Business Promotion Council). The organization provides its members with a variety of business opportunities that go beyond individual fields, such as robotic innovation (Figure 9.3). In addition, the New Energy and Industrial Technology Development Organization (NEDO), which is under the government's jurisdiction, is supporting the establishment of ethics and safety guidelines (NEDO, 2008). The National Institute of Advanced Industrial Science and Technology (AIST) is collaborating with robot manufacturers and universities to conduct research in Tsukuba city, which is a long-term care special zone. In addition, many related parties, particularly on university campuses, are being used for skills training for care workers. As in route 2 shown in Figure 8.2, some universities have established training courses for long-term care workers and are functioning as facilities to train certified care workers and social workers. Based on the rising need for long-term care, currently 179 universities have established such a course on campus (Table 9.2). As many of the teachers in these training facilities are qualified and experienced care workers,[2] this has the major benefit that these universities' researchers can use them to research detailed long-term care needs. Furthermore, in 2009, the government established an action plan to back up the activities of the METI (Table 9.3).

Table 9.2 Universities offering care/social work school in Japan

Area	Number of universities with care/social work schools
Hokkaido	8
Tohoku	13
Kanto	55
Koshinetsu	6
Hokuriku	2
Tokai	21
Kinki	34
Chugoku	16
Shikoku	6
Kyushu	16
Okinawa	2
Total	**179**

Source: Welfare and Medical Service Agency (2010a)

Table 9.3 Action plan to promote livelihood-support robots by Japanese government

2009–	*The livelihood-support robot project by METI (1.6 billion yen)*
2010–2011	Introductory period • Safety check (METI) • Risk assessment (METI) • Test at care facilities (METI, MHLW) • LTCI system maintenance for robot introduction (MHLW) • Test at special ward (e.g., Tsukuba city)
2012–2013	Primary introduction • Test of care worker robot (e.g., power suite) (METI, MHLW) • Power suit test with normal healthy subjects (METI) • Planning of mobility robots (related ministries)
2014–	Major introduction through business-to-business market • Implementation of robot-use promotion policy (MHLW) • Setting up robot assessment agency (METI) • Implementation of the telecommunication system for robot use (MPMHAPT)

Source: METI (2010)

Note: MPMHAPT means Ministry of Public Management, Home Affairs, Posts, and Telecommunications.

Through this initiative, many life-support robots are actually being used. The results of long years of research and development are starting to appear in a number of popular products, and to be exported overseas. Based on these successes, many companies are investing in developing life-support robots.

One leading example is HAL, a robot suit developed primarily by Professor Yoshiyuki Sankai of the University of Tsukuba. The HAL robot suit has functions to assist the wearer's movement. Bioelectric sensors attached to the skin monitor signals transmitted from the brain and control the robot suit (Sankai, 2006). With this suit, the wearer's physical capabilities are enhanced and in the case of care workers, they become able to lift care recipients easily. HAL has actually been introduced into hospitals and long-term care facilities in Japan, and there are a number of case studies, such as paralyzed elderly people being able to climb stairs wearing HAL.

One more example is the therapeutic robot PARO developed by AIST. PARO is designed to have positive psychological effects on the people it interacts with, as it responds to the calls of people and forms its personality from the provision of care. According to AIST (2006) and Wada *et al.* (2008), interacting with PARO improves brain function, as measured and analyzed in the brain waves of elderly patients with cognitive disorders. Robot therapy with PARO, therefore, might prevent cognitive disorders. In addition, the use of PARO might enhance the quality of care, making it possible to provide humane care. Takanori Shibata, Senior Research Scientist at AIST, states that "Elderly people with dementia, especially if their condition is severe, may get agitated and violent, and be unable to settle down. Previously, such patients were sedated, but if such patents have contact with PARO, they often settle down almost immediately. Although the use of PARO may not be 100 percent effective, it has no particular side effects" (Diginfonews, 2010). In Japan, as of 2010, 1,300 PARO robots have already been released, and the sales have been extended to overseas. Care facilities in Denmark and other European countries have started to introduce PARO. In the United States, PARO was certified by the Food and Drug Administration (FDA) as a medical product (Diginfonews, 2010).

In light of these trends, in 2010 METI announced that it expected the future growth in Japan's robot industry would be greatly dependent on the service field (Figure 9.4). Life-support robots will be a core part of the service field in the near future. In fact, it is estimated that the market for life-support robots will grow and by 2035 will constitute approximately 20 percent of the Japanese robot market worth 9.7 trillion yen (Table 9.4).

This market forecast is supported by a variety of private-sector surveys. According to the Japan Society for the Promotion of Machine Industry (2008), the life-support robots market could be worth 1.4534 trillion yen by 2030 (work use: 901.2 billion yen; home use 555.2 billion yen). In addition, while the Yano Research Institute (2013) forecast is more modest, it still expects the market to have become fully fledged from 2015 and the market for long-term care robots alone to have expanded to a scale of 34.98 billion yen by 2020. Furthermore, Seed Planning (2014) expects that the market for powered suits, which are mainly used in long-term care workplaces, will be worth more than 100 billion yen by 2024.

Table 9.4 Japanese robot industry market predictions (2015–2035) (detailed)

Division			Predicted market scale (billion yen)				Calculation
Major division	Middle division	Small division	2015	2020	2025	2035	
Manufacturing	Conventional industrial robot	–	936.5	1,052.4	1,092.6	1,102.7	Pattern 2
	Next-generation industrial robot	Assembly robot (Automobile)	32.4	99.2	239.3	798.8	Pattern 4
		Robot cell (Electric machine)	32.9	104.8	248.8	827.9	Pattern 4
Robot technology (RT) product	RT electric appliance/ home equipment	–	92.8	285.9	488.0	557.9	Pattern 5
	RT automobile	–	50.9	103.3	208.3	737.0	Pattern 5
	RT ship	–	15.9	28.1	44.4	72.9	Pattern 5
	RT railway	–	2.5	4.6	7.4	12.8	Pattern 5
	RT construction machine	–	14.9	29.8	57.6	175.0	Pattern 5
Agriculture, forestry, and fisheries	Agriculture	Land-use agriculture	1.1	2.3	7.3	27.6	Pattern 5
		Garden firming/ facility firming	0.9	3.9	15.0	92.7	Pattern 4
		Daily firming/ animal firming	10.2	29.4	49.8	58.8	Pattern 3
		Agriculture logistics	27.3	60.3	81.2	85.8	Pattern 3
	Forestry	–	1.7	8.4	30.4	87.2	Pattern 4
	Fisheries/ aquaculture	–	5.4	16.8	41.7	114.2	Pattern 4
Service	Medical care	Operational support	4.3	13.6	31.7	53.4	Pattern 3
		Pharmaceutical support	6.5	21.0	38.3	41.4	Pattern 3
	Long-Term Care	**Self-support**	**13.4**	**39.7**	**82.5**	**220.6**	Pattern 4
		Care support	**3.3**	**14.6**	**41.4**	**183.7**	Pattern 4

(Continued)

Table 9.4 (Continued)

Division			Predicted market scale (billion yen)				Calculation
Major division	Middle division	Small division	2015	2020	2025	2035	
	Healthcare	Fitness	137.6	146.1	157.6	181.7	Pattern 3
		Health monitoring	**5.4**	**16.1**	**44.0**	**148.0**	Pattern 3
	Room cleaning	—	**2.2**	**12.7**	**54.1**	**428.7**	Pattern 3
	Security	Machine security	21.0	61.0	124.9	268.9	Pattern 5
		Institutional security	1.7	21.0	70.3	163.2	Pattern 4
	Receptionist	—	0.2	0.9	3.9	46.5	Pattern 3
	Delivery	—	0.7	3.0	13.2	81.1	Pattern 3
	Transportation (business use)	—	**5**	**116.2**	**619.0**	**675.9**	Pattern 3
	Heavy-duty support	—	1.5	4.3	12.0	229.9	Pattern 3
	Food industry	Food handling	17.9	67.5	143.2	164.0	Pattern 3
		Food processing	8.1	30.5	79.3	174.3	Pattern 3
	Logistics	Palletizer/ depalletizer	21.2	41.0	86.5	152.3	Pattern 2
	Examination/ maintenance	House	4.6	9.8	15.7	21.3	Pattern 1
		Social infrastructure	21.6	103.8	218.8	180.5	Pattern 4
	Education	—	11.9	24.3	36.1	45.0	Pattern 1
	Amusement	—	21.1	35.7	57.6	122.2	Pattern 1
	Rescue	—	0.8	6.0	29.1	67.0	Pattern 1

Prospecting	–	1.7	7.3	25.7	81.1	Pattern 3
Transportation (home use)	–	**2.1**	**49.8**	**265.3**	**289.7**	Pattern 3
Hobby	–	22.3	71.6	1498.5	215.7	Pattern 1
House-keeping support	–	–	–	**15.7**	**85.8**	Pattern 3
MIMAMORI/communication	–	**0.3**	**1.1**	**3.6**	**34.1**	Pattern 3
Robot total		1,599.0	2,853.3	5,258.0	9,708.0	
Livelihood-support robot		**31.7**	**250.2**	**1,109.9**	**1,980.7**	
(occupancy rate in the total)		**(2%)**	**(8.8%)**	**(21%)**	**(20%)**	

Source: METI (2010)

Note: The bold text indicates the livelihood-support robot. The original source describes the number in increments of 100 million, but this table shows the number in increments of 1 billion. The term *MIMAMORI* is difficult to translate, but roughly, it means "to stand watch over frail elderly and/or small children and to offer help when necessary" in English.

Methodology: The prediction is calculated by the logistic curve model formed by the adoption number, household adoption rate, replacement cycle, and price transition of the anagogic (in terms of price and utilization) product in the past market of each division.

- Pattern 1: stochastics of the existing stochastics data
- Pattern 2: stochastics based on the existing market performance
- Pattern 3: stochastics based on the model curve of the anagogic robot
- Pattern 4: stochastics based on the market needs
- Pattern 5: stochastics based on the model curve of the anagogic RT product

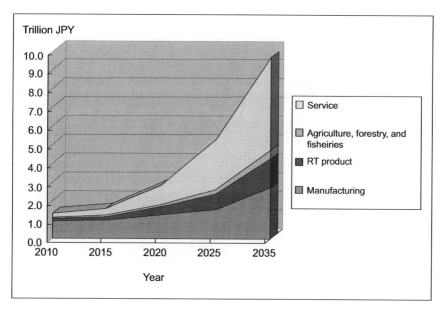

Trillion JPY

Legend:
- ☐ Service
- ▨ Agriculture, forestry, and fisheiries
- ■ RT product
- ▦ Manufacturing

Figure 9.4 Overall Japanese robot industry market prediction (2015–2035)
Source: METI (2010)
Note: RT indicates robot technology.

Moreover, it is possible that even the most optimistic forecast of market expansion is in fact still an under-evaluation. One reason is accelerating progress in artificial intelligence. It is claimed that in the next ten to 20 years, around half of the work performed by humans will be overtaken by machines. If this forecast is correct, even in the fields of long-term care and assisted living, in which relatively little progress is currently made in terms of measures to improve productivity, it is highly likely that the trend of mechanization will spread more than currently anticipated because of the high demand for it in advanced countries with aging populations. In particular, Japan accounts for around 30 percent of the world's industrial robot production (METI, "Results of the Robot Industry Market Trends Survey, 2013") and thereby has competitive advantages in artificial intelligence and robot technologies. Therefore, it is fully possible that the market will expand at a pace greatly exceeding that anticipated in current forecasts.

Another factor is the creation of legislation, which will support the market's expansion. Presently, there are growing voices for improvements in the working environment of care workers globally. As introduced in Chapter 7, according to the results of a survey in the United States, among all industries, care workers have the highest rate of workers' compensation due to injury, and legislation for this issue is being enacted in many countries. For example, in Australia, many care workers have back problems due to the task of assisting the movement of long-term care recipients, and thus, in 2008, in the wake of the "no-lifting policy" implemented by the Australian Nursing Association,[3] care workers were prohibited from lifting non-care workers and they became legally required to use a mobility crane robot. In fact, according to the Victorian Nurses Back Injury Prevention Project by the Ministry of Health, Labour and Welfare in Victoria, the no-lifting program has reduced the number of back injuries by 48 percent, reduced financial loss due to injuries by 74 percent, and reduced costs to deal with worker complaints by 54 percent. According to estimates by the Association for Technical Aids (2012), within the annual funding of approximately 930 million yen relating to care for the elderly in Victoria, Australia, the funds to purchase equipment, such as lifting equipment, actually constitutes more than 20 percent, at 200 million yen. If this development of improving the working environments of care workers spreads, it is extremely likely that it will spread to some long-term care facilities in Japan too, and the use of robots to assist care workers will take a dramatic leap forward on a global scale.

2. Source of industrial promotion

There is a need for financial support from the government for an industrial policy to ensure the sustainability of the CMM. In the previous section, an overview is provided of the mechanism for industrial promotion. In addition, it is essential to support industrial promotion, such as with subsidies and regulatory reform, to industrialize the responses to the care needs that have been ascertained. In the field of long-term care, in which demand is expected to increase rapidly in the context of declining birthrates and aging populations in advanced countries, Japan is the only country that is trying to find a path to promote industry in order to raise productivity. Indeed, among these countries, some, such as the United States, Germany, Switzerland, and South Korea, have competitive advantages in such fields as robots and mobility. To grow long-term care-related industries, urgent tasks are to utilize the experience of care workers to support research and development and field trials, and to promote the use of welfare equipment and robots, as well as to improve industrial productivity, and therefore, huge investment to achieve competitive advantage in the market is required to complete these tasks prior to the rivals.

However, although in general the shared recognition is that long-term care is an industrial growth field, cautious discussions have continued on financial support by governments; in other words, government financing is a problem.

Japanese government bonds had an outstanding balance of around 883 trillion yen, according to preliminary figures at the end of March 2015, which is close to 200 percent of GDP (Bank of Japan, 2015). Based on this, the Japanese government is in a state of financial crisis. Therefore, it is argued that as social security-related expenses are set to continue to increase, it will be difficult to increase public spending further in order to grow the long-term care-related industries. Indeed, at first glance this argument seems reasonable and valid.

However, in the first place, it is logically impossible for a such a country as Japan to default; Japan issues government bonds denominated in its own currency and has currency issuance rights in currencies other than its own, such as for the Eurozone, while the risk of the deterioration of government finances is limited to rising prices (inflation). Stiglitz (2012: 4) said the idea that [t]he state budget resembles the family budget is nothing more than a myth, explaining this as follows. During a recession when unemployment is high, if the state increases spending and supports the creation of demand, production expands and jobs are created. As a result, the amount of GDP increase will be several times the government expenditure amount, and tax revenues will increase. Thus, it is not necessary to worry about a government financial deficit.

In addition, currently, Japan is in a uniquely ideal environment for increasing public investment through issuing government bonds, as regardless of monetary policy, prices are barely rising (there is practically no inflation). First, there have been no price rises despite Japan's adoption of an ultra-low interest rate close to zero for many years, and in this interest rate climate, prices should rise, as, inherently, the purpose of companies is to maximize profits, and thus, they borrow funds for investment en masse. Next, particularly after the round of large-scale monetary easing in 2013, the Bank of Japan has targeted an inflation rate of around 2 percent, and even though the money stock has increased considerably, a rise in prices has barely been seen. An increase in the money stock damages the scarcity of money, and therefore, fundamentally, both companies and households should stop saving and undertake purchasing and investment. Despite this, prices have hardly risen at all. Moreover, recently, the government has been accumulating a balance of government bonds of up to around 200 percent of GDP; despite this, and contrary to fears about rising interest rates expressed by many economists and analysts, interest rates (yield) on government bonds have continued to fall, and have not risen even once (Figure 9.5).

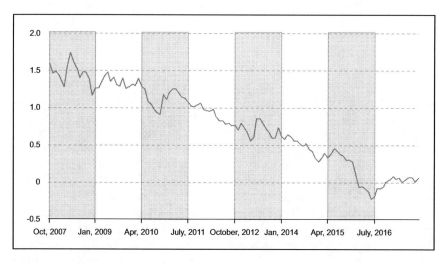

Figure 9.5 Interest rates of Japanese government bonds (10 years)
Source: Japan Bond Trading (2017)

The backdrop to this environment is economic deflation, which is different to inflation on which existing economics is premised. This phenomenon rarely occurs, happening "only once every few decades" (Koo, 2009), and characteristically it appears after the collapse of a bubble economy. In other words, today, companies and households that took on large amounts of debt due to investment from borrowing during the bubble period are "once bitten, twice shy" and have become excessively fearful about borrowing. Of course, if we consider each household and company from a micro viewpoint, the choice of not to borrow is not necessarily a bad one. There is also the idea that it is better not to borrow at all. However, if this were taken to the extreme and implemented collectively by many economic agents, the damage caused to the economy as a whole would be immeasurable. It would be, so to speak, a fallacy of composition. Even if the government were to implement policy to lower the interest rate, the "once bitten" households and companies still would not borrow, and even if the money stock were to increases, it would have practically no effect. Instead of borrowing, households and companies would rush to accumulate savings, and the banks' negative spread (for banks, deposits become liabilities with payment interest rates) increases unilaterally. For the banks, although they have an abundance of funds, there are no borrowers for them to lend to, and inevitably, they choose to purchase government bonds. As this happens all at once, the yield on government bonds steadily declines. This deflationary mechanism has been explained as "debt deflation" by Fisher (1933) up to the point of the fallacy of composition, and as "balance sheet recession" for the mechanism as a whole, including after that point, by Koo (2009, 2014).

Thus, is it possible that the yields on government bonds and treasury bills will rise in the future? The answer is of course "yes," but even if they do so, it would not seem to be that much of a problem. Due to deflation in the economy, the yield on government bonds declines even when large amounts of funds are being accumulated. About 95 percent of the holders of Japanese government bonds and treasury bills are domestic institutions and individuals, but the current situation is that they are unavoidably purchasing Japanese government bonds, as they are not lending funds for purposes other than this. If the Japanese economy escapes from the deflationary spiral (i.e., if demand recovers and lenders of funds to the private sector increase) the institutions and individuals that previously purchased government bonds might refrain from doing so, and instead lend funds to the private sector, which offers higher yields. In this case, the yield on government bonds will definitely rise. However, at the same time, government tax revenues will rise from the recovery in private-sector demand, and thus, the rate at which the government relies on the issuance of new government bonds will already have decreased considerably.

In response to the opinion that is strongly opposed to fiscal stimulus measures through the new issue of government bonds, in the final analysis, we observe that in recent years, government finances have become substantially fiscally sound. Figures 9.6 and 9.7 show the breakdowns of the holders of government bonds in 2011 and 2016, respectively. As these tables show, although the outstanding

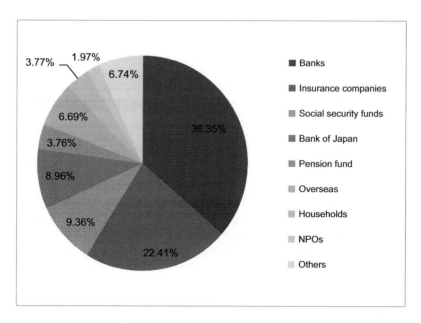

Figure 9.6 Share of Japanese government bonds holders (total: 755 trillion yen, March 2011)

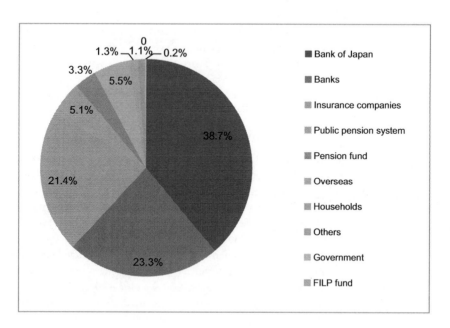

Figure 9.7 Share of Japanese government bonds holders (total: 959 trillion yen, December 2016)

balance of Japanese government bonds increased during this period from 755 trillion yen to 959 trillion yen, within this amount, the percentage of government bonds held by the Bank of Japan rose significantly, from 9 percent to slightly less than 39 percent. Of course, the increase in the percentage of government bonds held by the Bank of Japan was due to the monetary easing policy during that period (the issuance of large amounts of currency), which meant that the Bank of Japan purchased the government bonds held by private-sector banks. It is noteworthy that the Bank of Japan is the legally owned subsidiary of the Japanese government, which is owed the debt as named on the government bonds. In other words, the government bonds that are assets owned by the Bank of Japan and the government bonds that are debt for the Japanese government cancel each other out when consolidated. For the government, its own debt is recorded as an asset on the balance sheet of its wholly owned subsidiary, and so when combined with the corresponding assets of its subsidiary, this debt will in actual terms not exist on its consolidated balance sheet. Therefore, it is not necessary to repay it. Even though the outstanding balance of Japanese government bonds increased by around 204 trillion yen from 2011, the amount that it does not have to repay also rose from approximately 68 trillion yen to 374 trillion yen. In other words, the Japanese government's finances have become substantially sound at a pace exceeding the approximately 102 trillion yen increase in the outstanding balance of government bonds. If the Bank of Japan were to continue issuing large amounts of currency at the same pace, going forward, in just the next few years it would have purchased all of the government bonds on the market and in substantive terms, it would have achieved fiscal soundness. If it were to achieve this, sooner or later, it would be likely that the government would be required to steer a course from monetary easing to increasing the amount of government bonds issued alongside the fiscal stimulus measures. Of course, if during this period the economy changes direction and becomes inflationary, it might be difficult to continue to issue large amounts of currency and to increase the issuance of government bonds. However, in this case, fiscal soundness is realized inherently from the increase in tax revenues and private-sector investment is stimulated. Thus, in this scenario, even if the government did not invest a huge amount, it would still be possible for the long-term care-related industries to be promoted, as they would receive an abundance of private-sector funds. Whichever the case, at the very least, the Japanese government, in the current environment of a deflationary spiral, should not hesitate to conduct fiscal stimulus and invest huge amounts into industries that would seem almost certainly to be set for growth.

If the correct policies were to be implemented, the prospects for the Japanese long-term care market would be extremely bright. As described up to this point, the CMM is functioning in the market, if only one part of it. The first task is to increase the fields that meet the requirements of the CMM we have observed so far. Then, it is necessary to promote long-term care-related investment through public investment in maintaining and developing sufficient training for care workers on the front line, utilizing their knowledge to research and develop welfare equipment and robots, conducting demonstration experiment, and promoting their use. By aiming to provide the elderly with the best care in this way, a virtuous circle would be created that would lead to the sustainability of the CMM. To repeat this point, many market forecasts are certain that going forward for at least the next few decades, the long-term care market in practically all developed countries, including Japan and many countries in East Asia, will grow. It is possible that Japan, whose population is aging at a faster pace than anywhere else in the world, could lead the world in long-term care-related industries alongside its utilization of this market model.

3.   Issues for Japan's long-term care market

While overall, the prospects for Japan's long-term care market are bright, there are, of course, issues to be addressed. The primary issue is the thorough application of the CMM, which is the mechanism for service providers to constantly improve the quality of care. Up to this point, as verified in Chapter 4, we have observed the premise that users can select a group home based on the quality of care, because there is a mandatory external evaluation system in the group home market. However, in other markets, while there are systems for the mandatory disclosure of information on long-term care service and voluntary third-party evaluation services, there is no information that makes it possible to compare service quality, and thus, the fourth condition of the CMM, information publication, is not necessarily being met. The questions to be answered include which items on long-term care quality to actively include in a system to publish information on long-term care services, whether third-party evaluations should be compulsory, and whether to apply the external evaluation system used for group homes to other markets. Each of these questions requires some sorts of measures. Of course, this evaluation system ought to be applied to not only long-term care facilities, but also short-term care facilities using separately established indicators. In addition, the setting of the evaluation items should not be entrusted to each prefecture, but instead, it would be better if they were investigated toward the minimum items being unified across the country, and therefore, comparable. Certainly, nearly all of the prefectures use the evaluation items indicated by the Ministry of Health, Labour and Welfare, but there are also those, like Metropolitan Tokyo, that determine all of their evaluation items independently. In the LTCI system, essentially, the insurance covers the services within the municipality of the user's place of residence, and thus, users are unlikely to frequently compare the providers in different prefectures. However, from the perspectives of the significance of being able to compare regions and the national minimum, and the importance of the standardization of services as considered in the CMM, it would seem necessary to investigate increasing the commitment of the national government a little more. Moreover, even if the evaluation results were quantitative, it would be necessary to consider them from the viewpoint of the ease of analyzing the results. The results of the external evaluation used in Chapter 4 are extremely quantitative and are structured in a way so that it is easy to compare the providers and changes to the results. However, subsequent changes to the evaluation method have meant the external evaluation consists of self-evaluation, including somewhat subjective elements from the providers, and extremely qualitative comments from the external evaluators. The advantages of these changes are considered that it is easier for the service providers to use the comments from the external evaluators as advice, as if they were receiving consulting. However, in contrast to this advantage, these comments leave a lot of room for subjective evaluation by the evaluators as individuals. For people intending to use a service and other third parties (including researchers) who want to compare the quality of services from each provider, these changes have made this comparison more difficult. Because ability to compare the service providers is an essential element to continuously improve the quality of long-term care services in the market, it would be preferable if improvements were made in ensuring the objectivity of the evaluation items.

Next, relating to the standardization of long-term care services, is the task of further ensuring the objectivity of users' long-term care certification. According to Arami (2014), the responsiveness of long-term care certification is affected particularly by the involvement of the government's certification investigators. Currently, the occupancy rate in Japan's long-term care facilities is high, and in many cases, people do not have a place to receive long-term care, even if they want to receive it. In these instances, the long-term care certification can be affected by the vacancy conditions at the facilities receiving people and other administrative factors. In other words, originally, the certification to receive long-term care was to be based on an evaluation of the physical and mental state of the person who wished to receive this care, but in reality, it can be influenced by certain political factors. This situation needs to be improved in light of the principle of the standardization of long-term care services, according to which, necessary services must be provided to the people who need them. Resolving this issue will require guidance from certification investigators and other related parties, but this alone will not fundamentally solve the immediate issue of high occupancy rates at long-term care facilities. Therefore, it is important that remuneration for long-term care, which in recent years has been trending downward, is reversed and raised, thereby promoting the new market entry of long-term care providers. This can be expected to improve the excessively high occupancy rates at the facilities of long-term care providers and enable a return to the original intention of certification to receive long-term care.

The final task is to eliminate the shortage of care workers. In recent years, many people have commented loudly on this shortage of care workers, and as the government could not cover the demand for these workers domestically, it announced that it would be positively accepting foreign care workers from various other countries, including Indonesia and the Philippines. However, this policy is wrong on two points. First, this labor shortage is a shortage of people working in the field, not people with the skills to work in the field. As shown in Figure 9.7, for example, the number of registered certified care workers is trending upward, but of those, only around 60 percent are actually working in the field as certified care workers. In other words, despite having the skills to work in the field, more than 40 percent of these skilled people are not working in the field. According to Hanaoka (2011), wages are the major factor behind care workers leaving this field. Recently, remuneration for long-term care work has been gradually trending downward and it is highly possible that this has increased the number of people who are not working, even though they have the skills to do so. Stated another way, it seems possible that many of these people would return to the field if the wages for long-term care work increased. When considering the costs of recruiting care workers from other countries and having them study to learn Japanese and acquire Japanese qualifications, it would seem far more rational to encourage the return to work of these Japanese care workers who already have the skills to work in the field. Second, the knowledge acquired in the field by care workers on the front line, as described in Chapter 8, plays a guiding role in long-term care services, and as discussed in this chapter, is a fundamental asset essential for the promotion of long-term care-related industries. After having gone to the trouble to obtain this asset, care workers in Japan, compared to those from other countries who are highly likely to return to their home countries in the future, are much more likely to be utilized as assets within Japan. Thus, in the long term, from the perspective of utilizing the experience of care workers, the advantages of using domestic human resources are considerable. Therefore, the government should instead change to a policy of raising the wages of long-term care workers, thereby attracting to the long-term care industry talented human resources, including those with qualifications who are not currently working to return to work.

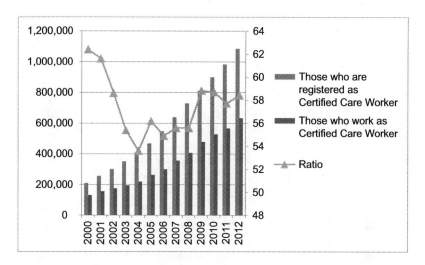

Figure 9.8 Ratio of certified care workers at work

4. Conclusion

In this chapter, industrial policy in order to ensure the sustainability of the CPM was discussed. First, it was shown that the increase in demand for long-term care, which tends to be seen as an increase in the financial burden on society, can be covered by improving productivity. Next, it was clarified that to achieve improving productivity, synergies should be generated between a high-level ability to understand the hidden needs for long-term care, which is a characteristic of Japanese care workers, and the robot technologies that already exist in Japan. In addition, industrial policies on these issues should be developed to a scale that can ensure the sustainability of the CPM. To meet the goals of industrial policies to ensure the sustainability of the CPM, it is important to raise wages for care work to secure excellent human resources over the long term at care work sites, and for the government first to actively invest in research and development in care-related industries.

Notes

1 The response rate for this survey was 96.5 percent. The reason for the high response rate was because it was a panel survey, but the relevant question was included only in the 2013 wave, and therefore, only the 2013 wave is used here.
2 Alternatively, they are people closely related to care workers.
3 However, prior to this in Victoria, a no-lifting policy had been in place from 1998 under the occupational health and safety management system.

10 Conclusion

"Managing the human service market" originating from Japan

This book investigated the mechanism to provide long-term care to respond to two unique features of human service: ambiguous policy goals and a considerable amount of frontline workers' discretion. The research analyzed how governments can address these two unique features to ensure a level of quality of human service above the minimum for their citizens, in the current situation in which diversifying needs and rapid increase in demand for long-term care place the provision of care in the hands of a competitive market.

The Introduction explained that many researchers have presented evidence that market utilization in the provision of human services is a necessary trend because governments today do not have the capacity to respond to provide human service directly. That chapter introduced yet another research stream that argues that market utilization itself causes long-term low-level quality service issues, because market competition means that some providers sacrifice quality for profit maximization.

By undertaking a survey of the history and theoretical research into human service provision through a competitive market, Chapter 1 defined two research questions to guide this book. In addition, it first outlined the reasons that governments need to be responsible for human service provision. Tracing the origin of human services, the research showed changes in government commitments to human service provision. The analysis concluded that today's democratic systems urge governments to ensure a certain standard of living for their people by being responsible for human service provision. Furthermore, the chapter investigated how human services are provided through a competitive market and how governments have tried to ensure care quality under competitive market conditions; the vehicle of analysis was the expanding and demanding example of long-term care.

To date, the literature primarily consists of two major points: (a) care market model to direct market competition to enhance the quality of care and (b) performance measurement to evaluate and regulate the providers' quality of care.

From that foundation, the first question hereafter was debated in Part I and the second question in Part II.

1 How should governments design the human service market in order to ensure service quality?
2 How should governments set performance measurement?

1. Part I Designing the human service market

Part I of this book presented and then tested a new market model, the CMM. The CMM seeks to overcome deficiencies in the existing market model, which allows the market to accommodate poor quality care. To this end, the CMM presents a theoretical market design in which quality of care is the sole basis for market competition. Therefore, by implementing the CMM as the ideal model, governments can direct market competition to enhance the quality of care and poor quality service is automatically eliminated from the market.

The CMM requires four preconditions: (a) a universal long-term care system; (b) standardized content of care according to care recipients' conditions; (c) no price competition; and (d) published care quality information.

The concept of the introduction of the CMM is as follows. First, as service provision is universal, those eligible receive the service by applying for a care needs evaluation. Second, since care content is standardized according to care recipients' conditions, users' care needs are assessed by official bodies and decisions regarding eligibility and levels of service are made based on individual conditions and care needs. Third, with the classification of care needs complete, users choose a provider. Since there is no price competition in the market, users choose a provider solely based on the service quality. However, due to the information asymmetry between users and providers in the human service market, official bodies must publish the providers' care quality information.

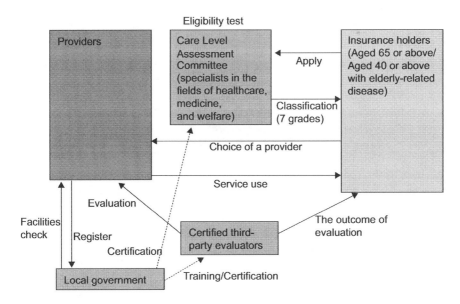

Figure 10.1 Flow chart of CMM

1.1.   The CMM is implementable

This book proved that the CMM is implementable. Surveying the long-term care markets in OECD nations, the research found that the Japanese LTCI market meets all four preconditions. Together with Japan, Austria, Germany, Luxemburg, Netherlands, Norway, Sweden, and South Korea meet the condition of universal care. Furthermore, Germany, Luxemburg, and South Korea clear the standardized content of care according to care recipients' conditions. However, Japan is the only country that meets the third condition: no price competition.

The confirmation of the CMM's implementability might make a positive impact on research into the market model in the field of health economics. For a long time, human service's market model in the field have been developed predominantly by experience and research in the United States. Almost all researched models assume a care system only for the economically vulnerable. The CMM is a new attempt to build a model based on the universal system and the experiences of Japan, the nation with the highest long-term care demands.

The current research identified two future research questions concerning this model. The first concerns its implementability in other countries. Some countries missed only two preconditions of CMM (i.e., no price competition and publishing providers' care quality information). Beside the publication of care quality information, for example, Germany missed the condition of no price competition, only because the care recipients can choose to receive cash-benefits, not in-kind care service (Naegele, 2009). That is, in the German long-term care market, the care recipients can even compare the care providers as consumer items. In this environment, certainly, the CMM does not properly direct market competition to enhance the quality of care. However, how such a deficit in the preconditions influences the efficacy of the model and how the CMM can be modified to overcome environments with deficits in only some conditions of the model are topics worthy of investigation. The second future question is about the applicability to other fields of human service. Since the CMM is designed to accommodate the ample discretion of human service providers, the model theoretically applies to all areas of human service. Nonetheless, each type of human service is empirically different. Analyzing other areas, such as childcare and homeless people's care, research can further develop the implementability of the CMM.

1.2.   The CMM is effective

The book endorsed that CMM is effective. A CMM assumption, that users choose a provider based on care quality, conflicts with information asymmetry models in the care market. However, the research proved that none of these conflicted models is fully supported, analyzing the case of group home providers in the Japanese LTCI market. Moreover, the research found that it is highly likely that the more competitive the market becomes, the better the quality of service that is provided, when governments (or other public bodies) publish the providers' care quality information.

The findings added empirical implications to the literature of care-related market's information asymmetry models: a) the contract failure model, (b) the medical arms race (MAR) model, and (c) Suzuki and Satake's (2001) model. First, although according to the contract failure model, users perceive non-profit providers as a sign of good service quality, this book proved there is no significant difference between non-profits and for-profits in overall service quality when users have access to providers' care quality information. In addition, the research further explained that the care service of non-profits tends to be better in care implementation, whereas for-profits tend to be better at interacting with care recipients' families. However, there are no significant differences in overall service quality. This suggests that the service quality of non-profits and for-profits might look different, depending on a person's point of view. Second, despite the concern of the MAR model, this book found that the CMM could direct market competition to enhance the providers' service quality. In fact, the service quality of the providers in competitive areas was significantly better than that of the providers in non-competitive (usually rural) areas, although the service quality of both areas' providers improved year by year. Third, Suzuki and Satake (2001) argued that providers newly entering the market lower the market's service quality, but this research found that the effect of Suzuki and Satake's (2001) model is very limited. Certainly, this research partly endorsed the model in that the service quality of new entrants is significantly worse than that of old entrants in the initial entry year. However, the research also found that the improvement of the new entrants' service quality was much greater than that of old entrants in the following year. This finding, then, suggests that the bad performance of the new entrants in the initial year is not necessarily because of the market's information asymmetry between users and providers, but because of the lack of care providing experience. As the new entrants in the initial year are inferior to the old entrants, especially on managerial indicators (see Chapter 4 for details), the research suggests that providers' management rather than care implementation requires experience.

Further studies of the findings should include application of the model to other human service markets. The current findings were based on the analysis of the Japanese group home market, in which the providers' care quality is the most comprehensively evaluated and published among the Japanese long-term care markets, due to the high ratio of care recipients with dementia in the market. The next step, therefore, is to investigate how the other markets, with a less strict evaluation, fulfill the information gap between users and providers in terms of providers' care quality.

1.3. *The CMM is financially sustainable*

The research suggested that the CMM is financially sustainable. Analyzing the long-term care expenses of OECD nations, the research revealed that universal systems are not necessarily more costly than means-tested systems. Investigating the merit good model and scale of economies, the research uncovered that the cost efficiency of universal systems was rooted in the small income gap of markets. This indicates that a small income gap is a precondition for the introduction of a universal system.

This finding serves as a basis for discussing whether governments should provide human services to all or to the economically vulnerable only. Since Esping-Andersen (1990) categorized nations according to the degree of human service (and social welfare) coverage, researchers have tended to seek differences in terms of nations' philosophy or politics. For example, Scandinavian nations are social democratic, because the people generally trust their governments, whereas the welfare policy of the United States is liberal, because of the strong individualism aspect of United States culture.[1] Although one might not disagree with these arguments, the findings of this book presented evidence of another cause for the different degrees of human service coverage: governments choose the degree of coverage based on the provision's efficiency in a market with a small income gap, and the service can easily be made uniform and mass-produced (i.e., scale of economies), whereas in a market with a large income gap, it is difficult to make the service uniform, and thus, the government must focus more on a target group (i.e., when the care system only for the economically vulnerable is more suitable[2]).

A limitation of the finding is its assumption that the service is socially demanded. As illustrated in Chapter 2, long-term care in OECD nations is in high demand and the trend is expected to continue for decades. Therefore, the finding of the correlation between the income gap and degree of human service coverage (only for the economically vulnerable or universal) is valid in this field of human service. However, the finding might not be applicable to some other fields of human service. For example, homeless support in OECD nations is in far less demand than long-term care. Regardless of the income gap, the governments are unlikely to apply universal systems for the provision of homeless support. In order to expand the generalizability of the finding, therefore, future research needs to investigate further the levels of demand that governments are required to decide between the universal system and the system for only the economically vulnerable.

1.4. The use of leverage improves the quality of long-term care

As the CMM is not applicable to a market in which there is a system only for the economically vulnerable, this book presented a quality improvement tool, which is applicable to this type of market. This tool takes advantage of leveraging other indicators, by finding the care quality indicator that has the most positive influence on other indicators. Positioning providers to focus their resources on improving that indicator is expected to improve the relevant quality indicator. Thus, governments would become able to improve service quality efficiently, regardless of differences in the care system.

This book proved that the CMM is implementable, effective, and financially sustainable. That is, the CMM sustainably directs market competition to enhance the quality of service along with the care quality indicators approved by governments. The remaining question was how to measure providers' care quality. This question was answered in Part II.

2. Part II Process-based performance measurement model: reflecting users' needs in human service

As Part I proved, governments could direct market competition to enhance the market's care quality by implementing the CMM. Part II investigated the remaining question: how does one measure quality of care? The research began by comparing current outcome-based performance measurement and the alternative process-based performance measurement. The comparison found weaknesses in both measurements: process-based performance measurement is not applicable to the current market-utilizing public policy model, and outcome-based performance measurement does not fit the ambiguous policy goals of human service. However, the weakness of process-based performance measurement is compensable, whereas the weakness of outcome-based performance measurement is crucial in terms of ensuring the quality of human service. Favoring the alternative process-based performance measurement, this book modified the market utilizing public policy model for the use of process-based performance measurement.

This book then presented and tested the process-based performance measurement with the care policy model (CPM) (i.e., process-based performance measurement model). The process-based performance measurement model seeks to reflect users' needs in the care service by promoting the interaction between governments and providers who know the best about users' needs. To this end, the process-based performance measurement model requires the input of providers' behavior and the output of providers' training.

The required modification of the current market-utilizing CPM can be described, using the logic of governance of Lynn *et al.* (2000). Adding the element of care workers' behavior to the current model achieved the necessary modification.

The process-based performance measurement model can be described as follows: the policy outcomes depend on governance in that governments (or public bodies) a) grasp public needs by observing the social environment; (b) set up the treatment (performance measurement) based on client characteristics and care workers' behavior; (c) build the structure of the market outsourcing of human service provision to non-government sectors with trained care workers; and (d) finally, manage the human service market.

2.1. Process-based performance measurement model reflects users' needs

This book found that the process-based performance measurement model reflected users' needs in care service. Although this is very important, the existing outcome-based performance measurement has missed the chance to recognize users' needs. Focusing on the outcomes, in outcome-based performance measurement, governments do not interact with providers (care workers), who know the best about users' needs. Unlike many other public services, recipients of human service often cannot present their needs properly (e.g., elderly with dementia). Connecting between governments and providers, however, the process-based performance measurement model allows governments to grasp the users' needs and to ensure their reflection in service by measuring and training the behavior of care workers.

This finding reinforces the concept of Lipsky's (1980) "system of street-level bureaucrats" in the human service market. In the era of the traditional public bureaucracy model scheme, Lipsky (1980) asserted the importance of human service's frontline workers, named "street-level bureaucrats," because they inevitably had a considerable amount of discretion in providing the service. As the provision of human services has been outsourced to non-government sectors, however, governments have gradually lost the connection with frontline workers. As Lynn *et al.*'s (2000) logic of governance shows, such a connection has become unnecessary in the outsourcer–outsourcee relationship. Nonetheless, the human service feature of front-line workers' discretion is unchanged. Missing the connection with frontline workers who know the best about users' needs, governments have faced a long-term care quality issue in the human service market. This book revealed the mechanism of reflecting users' needs in the service (and/or performance measurement) and suggested the use of the process-based performance measurement model.

For further research of this model, it was necessary to investigate its applicability and financial sustainability. Although the model theoretically reflects users' needs in the measurement, questions remained. a) How can governments connect with care workers? (b) How should governments train care workers? (c) How can governments ensure the financial sustainability of care workers' training, which tends to be costly as the number of care workers increases? These questions were answered in the findings summarized as follows.

2.2. *Achieving interactions with care workers*

Analyzing primarily the case of Japan, this book found that securing a connection with care workers could be achieved by giving them career path advantages to be involved in the process of performance measurement. In Japan, experience being a care worker is either necessary or very advantageous to participate in the process of setting performance indicators, implementing the measurement, and, if the market applies the CMM, classifying the care recipients' care needs. With this system, the setting and implementation of process-based performance measurement always reflects the voices of frontline workers.

This system benefits not only governments, but also care workers. Although the salaries of care workers might not be satisfactory, career paths to be able to make decisions in the policymaking process motivate them and attract capable human resources. As the OECD survey indicated (see Table 7.9), recruiting a competent work force is commonly a major concern of governments. The system benefits both governments and providers.

This finding has implications for the debate on how to listen to the voices of the socially vulnerable. In most cases, human service users are socially vulnerable and often incapable of exercising the consumer's right of complaint. As Lipsky (1980) claimed, their voices are unlikely understood by top-floor executives involved in policymaking. The finding presents a model for governments to listen to the voices of the socially vulnerable through frontline (street-level) workers.

The remaining question related to this finding was how governments could trust these frontline workers. As these workers might take on very important roles of human service provision, governments need to ensure the quality of care workers. Certainly, the career path advantages for care workers attract capable human resources. However, that does not assure their qualification for representing users' voices, and eventually, reflecting them in policy. The next issue, then, was how to train care workers.

2.3. *Care workers' training to uncover hidden needs*

This book found that care workers' training needs to cover communication skills to uncover hidden users' needs, and identified two phases of care workers' training. Phase 1 training is to assure appropriate care implementation. Focusing on physical skills, governments train to ensure the safety of care implementation, such as care recipients' physical transfer. This training also protects care workers from injuries, including back pain. The purpose of Phase 2 training extends to strategies and skills to discover care recipients' hidden care needs. Valuing care workers' communication skills, governments train care workers to be able to respond not just to visible care needs, but to invisible needs as well. This training helps care workers have capacity to present care recipients' hidden needs to governments. In addition, understanding care recipients through communication training protects care workers from becoming emotionally drained.[3] The purpose of the process-based performance measurement model is not only to ensure the implementation of care service, but also to pick up hidden care needs. Therefore, the required training for the model is Phase 2 training.

This book identified the training required for the process-based performance measurement model. As the model expects care workers to respond to visible and hidden service needs, Phase 2 training is necessary. This finding is among the first to identify the required training content for utilizing the concept of "street-level" representation in human service provision.

The remaining question was the financial sustainability of Phase 2 training. The research showed that Phase 2 training required far more training hours than Phase 1 training. The needs of human service, particularly long-term care, are expected to increase. The cost of the training could be a serious concern in the provision of service.

2.4.   *Sustainability of training*

This book found that governments could ensure the suitability of care workers' training by aiming for the best possible human service. Analyzing the case of Japan, the research discovered that hidden care needs uncovered by trained care workers boosted the national economy. That is, care workers' efforts to provide the best possible service elicited potential service needs and industries responded to these needs. For example, the Japanese government predicts that the life-support robot industry will play an important role in boosting the value of the robot industry to 9.7 trillion yen by 2035 (METI, 2010).

This finding impacts the discussion of increasing human service needs. For some time, increasing human service needs have been perceived rather negatively, because they create a lot of public expense. As discussed in Chapter 2, one of the key factors behind the shift in the policy model to market utilization was to ease this financial burden. Certainly, the finding from the Japanese case does not decrease the expense, but increases it. Highlighting the positive social effects of increasing human service needs, however, the experiences of Japan provide a mechanism to make the service provision sustainable. That is, the more training of care workers there is, the more hidden needs are uncovered. Then, the elicited needs boost the economy. Importantly, the collaboration among governments, providers, and industries benefit them all, bringing financial sustainability for governments,[4] better care for providers,[5] and new business for industry. Certainly, connecting elicited long-term care needs and the robot industry might be rather unique to Japan. However, the principle of market economy that elicited needs to stimulate industrial activities is applicable to every market.

For further research of this finding, multidisciplinary research might be required. To strike a balance between market contestability and service quality assurance by this finding, the research would seem to need to include several views, such as economics (business), engineering, medicine (nursing), and public policy.

An additional contribution of this book is its review of the case of Japanese human service. The process-based performance measurement model takes a bottom-up approach in that the model values the role of frontline workers. This approach has been actively researched in the field of business as Japanese-style management, especially after Vogel (1979) conceptualized it. Unlike the field of business, however, Japanese-style management in the field of human service has been greatly overlooked. Even when Lipsky (1980) claimed the importance of frontline workers ("street-level bureaucrats," in his words) in human service, few studies mentioned the case of Japan. Such bottom-up approaches in human service provision gradually lost attention,[6] in fact, as the market-utilization public policy model became popular in the provision of human service. Nonetheless, the importance of such a bottom-up approach is unchanged, because the provision of human services still needs a considerable amount of frontline workers' discretion. The Japanese case is, therefore, important, not only because Japan has faced the most radical increase of long-term care needs, but also because Japanese style management has many implications for the provision of human service. An additional contribution of this book is that it addresses the absence of the Japanese case in the research of human service provision.

3. Summary

This book proved that governments could reflect users' needs in the human service market by introducing the process-based performance measurement model. Connecting the measurement model to the CMM presented in Part I, the long-term quality issue in the human service market is solved.

The models in this book respond to two unique features of human service: ambiguous policy goals and a considerable amount of frontline workers' discretion. Therefore, the models are applicable to other fields of human service (i.e., childcare and homeless support). However, the empirical value of these potential models needs further research, because the context of these areas is different from that of long-term care.

4. Implications of the public policy model utilizing the market

The nature of human service is different from that of other public services. As repeatedly mentioned in this book, a considerable amount of service providers' (i.e., care workers') discretion and the ambiguous policy goals are distinctive characteristics of human service. Despite this, the existing market-utilizing, public policy model treats human service the same as other public services in terms of provision through a competitive market. Throughout the book, this research suggested that such treatment has actually caused the long-term care quality issue. This research studied an alternative model for human service provision through a competitive market and, in turn, the impact on the existing public policy model. The findings of this research can be summarized in a simple claim that recurs throughout this book, as follows.

As the nature of human service is different from that of other public services, the existing market model and public policy model used in the market provision of other public services are not directly applicable to the market provision of human service.

This section examines the implications of these research findings for the current literature on the public policy model and identifies some avenues for future research. In doing so, this section shows that the research undertaken in this book contributes to current knowledge about the public policy model and about public service provision in a competitive market.

5. Reconciling service quality assurance to human service provided through the market

In reviewing existing studies of the public policy model, Chapter 2 identified that public service provision through the market is not fully supported due to concerns about service quality assurance. Certainly, some public services, including telecommunications, delivery, and public transportation, are successfully provided through the market in that they do not usually sacrifice service quality over competition. These successes are, however, only because the quality of these services is heavily standardized and, in turn, the purchasing model works as $\Upsilon = xp$ (i.e., competing services of the same quality for better efficiency). In the fields of human service, on the other hand, the quality is not uniform, because each service needs to be customized for a user. As a result, the purchasing model becomes $\Upsilon = x \ (p, \ q)$, which accommodates a poor quality but inexpensive good as well as a good quality but expensive good in the market. In addition, it is difficult to measure the quality of service due to ambiguous policy goals. The information asymmetry models (i.e., contract failure model, MAR model, and Suzuki and Satake's, 2001 model) also support the difficulty of the measurement.

Nonetheless, this book proved that such service quality issues could be solved. Implementing the CMM, governments can direct competition to enhance the service quality. Care performance can be measured by the process-based performance measurement model. The information gap between users and providers can be bridged by making the care quality information (i.e., the outcome of the performance measurement) available to the public. Under these conditions, these findings support the use of a competitive market in the provision of public care services.

In summary, this book supports the market use of human service provision, but the research suggests that the market and public administration theory is not indelibly written. As each type of public service has distinguishing features, the market model and public policy model need to adjust continuously to the changing needs in each type of service.

Notes

1 In fact, Esping-Andersen (1990) himself analyzed the differences in terms of history and/or political attitude.
2 As an aside, this might even be extended to explain the healthcare issue: why the United States government has been struggling to introduce a universal healthcare system.
3 As discussed in Chapter 8, care workers inevitably face some very dramatic stages of care recipients' emotions.
4 The size of human service expense is usually compared by the expense-to-GDP ratio (see Table 1.2, for example). Although the expense is increased, the related GDP growth offsets the increase.
5 This, of course, benefits users as well, because the supply is originally the response to their needs.
6 This does not mean that Lipsky's (1980) work has lost attention. His idea has still been actively quoted in various fields in public administration, but not in the role of frontline workers in the field of human service provision.

References

AIST (2007). *Seikatsu-shien robotto no sangyou-ka nimukete (Industrialising the Livelihood Support Robot).* <http://rd.kek.jp/slides/20070221/rtm.pdf>

AIST (2006). *Paro Found to Improve Brain Function in Patients with Cognition Disorders.* <www.parorobots.com/pdf/pressreleases/Paro%20found%20to%20improve%20Brain%20Function.pdf>

Albrow, M. (1970). *Bureaucracy.* Pall Mall Press, London.

Amano, T. (2014). *Obama no iryo kaikaku (Obama's Medical Reform).* Keisou shobou.

Arami, R. (2014). Shikakunintei no jisshikatei niokeru akutaa no outousei no kiteiyouin to sono mekanizumu (Decision making factors and its mechanism of care grade classification). *Shakaikagakukenkyu,* Vol. 65 (1): 1–44.

Asada, T. (2013). *Toshibu niokeru ninchisho yuubyouritu to nintishou no seikatukinou shougai heno taiou (The Prevalence Rate of Dementia in Urban Area and the Support to the Patients' Activities of Daily Living).* <www.tsukuba-psychiatry.com/wp-content/uploads/2013/06/H24Report_Part1.pdf>

Association for Technical Aids (2012). *Koshi wo itame nagi kaigo and kaigo (Nursing and Care Not for Damaging the Back).* <www.techno-aids.or.jp/research/vol15.pdf>

Aulich, C., Halligan, J., and Nutley, S. (2001). *Australian Handbook of Public Sector Management.* Allen & Unwin, Sydney.

Australian Institute of Health and Welfare (1995). *Australia's Welfare: Services and Assistance.* Australian Government Publishing Service (AGPS), Canberra.

Bank of Japan (2015). *Shikin junkan (Money Flow).* <www.boj.or.jp/statistics/sj>

Bates-Jensen, B. M., *et al.* (2003). The minimum data set pressure ulcer indicator: Does it reflect differences in care processes related to pressure ulcer prevention and treatment in nursing homes. *Journal of the American Geriatrics Society,* Vol. 512: 1203–1212.

Behn, D. R. (2003). Rethinking accountability in education: *How* should *who* hold *whom* accountable for *what? International Public Management Journal,* Vol. 6 (1): 43–73.

Ben-Ner, A. (2002). The shifting boundaries of the mixed economy and the future of the nonprofit sector. *Annals of Public and Cooperative Economics,* Vol. 1: 5–40.

Berenson, R. A., Bodenheimer, T., and Pham, H. H. (2006). Specialty-service lines: Salvos in the new medical arms race. *Health Affairs,* Vol. 25 (5): 337–343.

Boston, J. (1991). The theoretical underpinnings of public sector restructuring in New Zealand, in Boston, J., Martin, J., Pallot, J., and Walsh, P. (eds), *Reshaping the State: New Zealand's Bureaucratic Revolution.* Oxford University Press, Auckland.

Boyne, G. A. (1996). The intellectual crisis in British public administration: Is public management the problem or the solution? *Public Administration*, Vol. 74: 679–694.

Braithwaite, J. (2001). The challenge of regulating care for older people in Australia. *BMJ*, 2001, Vol. 323: 443–446.

Budget Bureau, the Ministry of Finance (2014). *Shakaihoshou 1 (Social Security 1).* <www.mof.go.jp/about_mof/councils/fiscal_system_council/sub-of_fiscal_system/proceedings/material/zaiseia281004/01.pdf>

Bureau of Labor Statistics (2010). *Occupational Outlook Handbook 2010–11 Edition.* <www.bls.gov/oco.htm>

Burns, T., and Stalker, G. M. (1961). *The Management of Innovation.* Tavistock, London.

Calvin, J. (1536). *Institute of the Christian Religion: Christian Classics External Library.* <www.ccel.org/ccel/calvin/institutes.html>

Care Work Foundation (2008). *Kaigoroudousha ni taisuru shisaku no genjo (Policies on Care Workers).* <http://ns1.kaigo-center.or.jp/report/pdf/h20_kenkyukai_3.pdf>

Castles, G. F., *et al.* (2010). *The Oxford Handbook of the Welfare States.* Oxford University Press, Oxford.

Certified *Social Worker and Certified Care Worker's Law (Shakaifukushi-shi oyobi Kaigofukushi-shi hou) of 1987.* Government of Japan. <www.law.e-gov.go.jp/htmldata/S62/S62HO030.html>

Choi, J. (2009). *1Training System of Care Workers in Long-Term Care System and Quality of Care Services in Korea: From the Viewpoint of First Launching LTC Insurance.* The 19th International Association of Gerontology and Geriatrics (IAGG) Congress 2009, July 5–9th, 2009, Paris.

CMS (2010). *Public Quality Indicator and Resident Report.* Centers of Medicare and Medicaid Services, the United States Department of Health and Human Services.

Cohen, J., and Spector, W. (1996). The effect of Medicaid reimbursement on quality of care in nursing homes. *Journal of Health Economics*, Vol. 15: 23–48.

Crozier, M. (1964). *The Bureaucratic Phenomenon.* University of Chicago Press, Chicago.

Cutler, D. M. (1996). Why don't markets insure long-term risk? *Harvard University and National Bureau of Economic Research, Working Paper*, Cambridge, MA.

Cutler, D. M., and Maera, E. (2001). Change in the age distribution of mortality over the 20th century. *National Bureau of Economic Research, Working Paper No. 8556*, Cambridge, MA.

Davidson, B. (2009). For-profit organizations in managed markets for human services, in King, D., and Meagher, G. (eds), *Paid Care in Australia: Politics, Profits, Practices.* Sydney University Press, NSW.

Devers, K. J., Brewster, L. R., and Cassalino, L. P. (2003). Changes in hospital competitive strategy: A new medical arms race? *Health Service Research*, Vol. 38 (12): 447–469.

Diginfonews (2010). *PARO Therapeutic Baby Harp Seal Robot.* <www.diginfo.tv/2010/08/12/10-0138-r-en.php>

Donabedian, G. (1987). Commentary on some studies on the quality of care. *Health Care Financing Review*, Spec No: 75–85.

Dranove, D., Shanley, M., and Simon, C. (1992). Is hospital competition wasteful? *Rand Journal of Economics*, Vol. 23 (2): 247–262.

Dubois, P. (1979). *Sabotage in Industry*. Penguin Books, Harmondsworth.

Dunleavy, P., and O'Leary, B. (1987). *Theories of the State*. Macmillan, London.

Dusansky, R. (1989). On the economics of institutional care of the elderly in the US: The effects of change in government reimbursement. *Review of Economics*, Vol. 56: 141–150.

Ellwood, J. (2000). Prospects for the study of the governance of public organizations and policies, in Heinrich, C., and Lynn, L., Jr. (eds), *Governance and Performance: New Perspectives*. Georgetown University Press, Washington, DC.

Endo, H. (2006). *Iryo to hieirisei, hoken, iryoteikyo seido (Medicaid Patients, and the Quality of Nursing Home Care)*. Funso Shobo Publishing, 47–79.

Endo, H. (1995). Iryo fukushi niokeru eirisei to hieirisei (For-profits and nonprofits in care industry). *Iryo to shakai*, Vol. 5 (1): 27–41.

Esping-Andersen, G. (1990). *The Three Worlds of Welfare Capitalism*. Polity Press, Cambridge and Princeton University Press, Princeton.

Farley, D. E. (1985). Competition among hospitals: Market structure and its relation to utilization, costs, and financial position: Hospital studies program. *National Center for Health Service Research and Health Care Technology Assessment, Research Note 7, 1985*, U.S. Department of Health and Human Services, National Center for Health Service Research and Health Care Technology,.

Feng, Z. D., Grabowski, D. C., Intrator, O., and Mor, V. (2006). The effect of state Medicaid case-mid payment on nursing home resident acuity. *Health Service Research*, Vol. 41 (4 Pt. 1): 1317–1336.

Fisher, I. (1933). The debt-deflation theory of great depression. *Econometrica*, Vol. 1 (4): 337–357.

Frederickson, G. H., and Smith, B. K. (2003). *The Public Administration Theory Primer*. Westview Press, CO, Boulder, U.S.A.

Fries, B. E., *et al.* (1997). Effect of the national resident assessment instrument on selected health conditions and problems. *Journal of the American Geriatrics Society*, Vol. 45: 994–1001.

General Insurance Association of Japan (2002). *Songai hoken ni kannsuru zenkoku chousa sougou houkokusho (National Comprehensive Report Regarding Insurance)*. General Insurance Association, Tokyo.

Gertler, P. J. (1992). Medicaid and the cost of improving access to nursing home care. *Review of Economics and Statistics*, Vol. 74 (2): 338–345.

Gertler, P. J. (1989). Subsidies, quality, and the regulation of nursing home. *Journal of Public Economics*, Vol. 38: 33–52.

Gertler, P. J. (1984). *Structural and Behavioural Differences in the Performance of Proprietary and Not-for-Profit Organization*. Mimeo.

Gertler, P. J., and Waldman, D. M. (1992). Quality-adjusted cost functions and policy evaluation in the nursing home industry. *Journal of Political Economy*, Vol. 100 (6): 1232–1256.

Gomez-Ibanez, J., and Meyer, J. (1993). *Going Private: The International Experience with Transport Privatization*. Brookings Institution Press, Washington, DC.

Hakit21 (2010). *Kaigonintei Shinsakai towa? (What Is CLAC?)*. Local Care Information System, Hyogo Prefectural Government, Japan. <www.hakit21.ne.jp/system/main15.htm>

Hanaoka (2011). Kaigo roudousha no rishoku youin (Care staff turnover in long-term care services for older people). *Japanese Journal of Health Economics and Policy*, Vol. 23 (1): 39–57.

Hansmann, H. (1980). The role of nonprofit enterprise. *Yale Law Journal*, Vol. 89 (5): 835–901.

Harrington, C. (2001). Regulating nursing homes: Residential nursing facilities in the United States. *BMJ*, September: 507–510.

Hawes, *et al.* (1997). The OBRA-87 nursing home regulations and implementation of the resident assessment instrument: Effects on process quality. *Journal of the American Geriatrics Society*, Vol. 45: 977–985.

Health and Welfare Statistics Association, Japan (2007). *Toukei de wakaru kaigohoken (Statistics of Long-Term Care Insurance)*. Ministry of Health, Labour, and Welfare, Government of Japan, Tokyo.

Heinrich, C., and Lynn, L., Jr. (2000). *Governance and Performance: New Perspectives*. Georgetown University Press, Washington, DC.

Hersch, P. L. (1984). Competition and the performance of hospital markets. *Review of Industrial Organization*, Vol. 1 (4): 324–340.

Hirth, R. (1999). Consumer information and competition between nonprofit and for-profit nursing homes. *Journal of Health Economics*, Vol. 18: 219–240.

Hood, C. (1991). A public management for all seasons? *Public Administration*, Vol. 69: 3–19.

Hotta, S. (2012). Care juujisha kakuho ni muketa shokadai (The issues on employing care workers). *ShakaihoshoKenksyu*, Vol. 47 (2): 382–400.

Hughes, O. (1998). *Public Management and Administration*. Macmillan, Melbourne.

Institute of Medicine (IOM) (1986). *Improving the Quality of Care in Nursing Homes*. National Academy Press, Washington, DC.

James, E., and Rose-Ackerman, S. (1986). *The Nonprofit Enterprise in Market Economics*. Harwood Academic Publishers, London.

Japan Bond Trading (2017). *Kokusai chokikinri suii 10nen (The Interest Rates of Japanese Government Bonds, 10 Years)*. <www.bb.jbts.co.jp/marketdata/market-data01.html>

Japanese Association of Certified Care Workers (2005). *Kaigofukushi-shi no Jittai chousa (A Survey of Certified Care Workers)*. Japanese Association of Certified Care Workers, Tokyo.

Japan Society for the Promotion of Machine Industry (2008). *RT ni yoru sangyou hakyuu-kouka to shijou-bunseki nikansuru chousa (Market Research on Industrial Ripple Effect by Robot Technology)*. Japan Robot Association, Tokyo.

Kadoya, Y. (2011). Kaigo saabisu no shitu kaizen no mechanism (The mechanism of quality-improvement of long-term care service). *Japanese Journal of Social Welfare*, Vol. 51 (4): 128–138.

Kadoya, Y. (2010). Managing the long-term care market: The constraints of service quality improvement. *Japanese Journal of Health Economics and Policy*, Vol. 21 (E1): 247–264.

Kasuno, K. (1997). *The History and Theory of Social Welfare: From Elizabeth Poor Law to Social Security*. Nishi-nihon Publishing (in Japanese), Tokyo.

Kawamura, M. (2008). *Kaigo Kaigo-roudou chousa-kenkyu project 1 cyuukan-houkoku (Care Labour Force Survey Research Project 1 Intermediately-Report).* <www.econ.hokkai-s-u.ac.jp/~masanori/2008.09kaigo00>

Kessler, D. P., and McClellan, M. B. (1999). Is hospital competition socially wasteful? *National Bureau of Economic Research, Working Paper No.7266*, Cambridge, MA.

Kettl, D. (2000). *The Global Public Management Revolution: A Report on the Transformation of Governance.* Brookings Institution Press, Washington, DC.

Kettl, D. (1993). Public administration: The state of the field, political science, in Finifter, A. (ed), *The State of the Discipline.* The American Political Science Association, Washington, DC.

Kettl, D. (1988). *Government by Proxy: (Mis) Managing Federal Programs.* Congressional Quarterly Inc., Washington, DC.

Knichman, J. R., and Snell, E. K. (2002). The 2030 problem: Caring for aging Baby Boomers. *Health and Experimental Research*, Vol. 37 (4): 849–884.

Koo, C. R. (2014). *The Holy Grail of Macroeconomics: Lessens from Japan's Great Recession.* Wiley.

Koo, C. R. (2009). *The Escape from Balance Sheet Recession and the QE Trap: A Hazardous Road for the World Economy.* Wiley.

Kübler-Ross (1969). *On Death and Dying.* Touchstone, New York.

Landau, M. (1973). On the concept of a self-correcting organization. *Public Administration Review*, Vol. 33 (6): 536.

Lane, J.-E. (1993). *The Public Sector: Concepts, Models and Approaches.* Sage Publications, London.

Li, L., and Ziemba, R. (2009). *Direct Care Workers in the United States: Challenges in Recruitment, Retention and Training.* The 19th International Association of Gerontology and Geriatrics (IAGG) Congress 2009, July 5–9th, 2009, Paris.

Li, W., and Xu, L. (2004). The impact of privatization and competition in the telecommunications sector around the world. *Journal of Law and Economics*, Vol. 47 (2): 395–430.

Life Insurance Association of Japan (2002). *Seimeihoken jigyou gaiikyo (Outline of Insurance Business).* <www.seiho.or.jp/data/statistics/index.html>

Lipsky, M. (1980). *Street-Level Bureaucracy.* Russell Sage Foundation, New York.

Luft, *et al.* (1986). The role of specialized clinical services in competition among hospitals. *Inquiry*, Vol. 23: 83–94.

Luther, M. (1520). *To the Christian Nobility of the German Nation: Religious Encyclopaedia.* <www.ccel.org/ccel/luther/first_prin.v.i.html?highlight=to,the,christian,nobility,of,german,nation#highlight>

Lynn, L., Jr., Heinrich, C., and Hill, C. (2001). *Improving Governance: A New Logic for Empirical Research.* Georgetown University Press, Washington, DC.

Lynn, L., Jr., Heinrich, C., and Hill, C. (2000). Studying governance and public management: Challenges and prospects. *Journal of Public Administration Research and Theory*, Vol. 10 (2): 233–261.

Lynn, L., Jr., Heinrich, C., and Hill, C. (1999). *The Empirical Study of Governance: Theories, Models, Methods.* Presented at the Workshop on Models and Methods for the Empirical Study of Governance, April 23th–May 1st, 1999, University of Arizona, Tucson, Arizona.

Mankiw, G. N. (2014). *Principle of Microeconomics* (7th ed.). Sengage Learning.

Megginson, W. L., and Netter, J. M. (2001). From state to market: A survey of empirical studies on privatization. *Journal of Economic Literature*, Vol. 39 (2): 321–369.

Mehdizadeh, S., and Applebaum, R. (2005). A review of nursing home resident characteristics in Ohio. *Scripps Gerontology Center Report Series*. 1–18.

Merton, R. (1952). Bureaucratic structure and personality, in Merton, R., *et al.* (eds), *Reader in Bureaucracy*. Free Press, Glencoe, III, NY.

METI (2010). *2035nen ni muketa robotto sangyou no shourai shijou yosoku (Market Forecast of Robot Industry in 2035)*. <www.meti.go.jp/press/20100423003/20100423003-2.pdf>

METI (2009). *Sangyou kouzou bijon 2010 (Industrial Structure Vision 2010)*. <www.meti.go.jp/committee/summary/0004660/index.html>

MHLW (2015). *Dai 26 kai kaigofukushishi kokkashiken goukakuhappyou (The Results of the 26th National License Exam of Certified Care Worker)*. <www.mhlw.go.jp.stf/houdou/0000041173.html>

MHLW (2014). *Shakaifukushihi no tourokushasuu no suii (The Numbers of Registered Certified Care Workers)*. <www.mhlw.go.jp/bunya/seikatsuhogo/shakai-kaigo-fukushi3.html>

MHLW (2010a). *Kongo no kaigo jinzai ikusei no arikata ni kannsuru kentoukai chuukan matome (Interim Summary of the Investigation Commission on Care Worker's Training)*. <www.mhlw.go.jp/stf/houdou/2r9852000000jxj2-img/2r9852000000kg8o.pdf>

MHLW (2010b). *Kaigo fukushi-shi no gaiyou (Overview of Certified Care Worker)*. <www.mhlw.go.jp/general/sikaku/25.html>

MHLW (2010c). *Kaigohoken seido ni kansuru kokumin no minasama karano goi-kenbosyu (Public Opinion on Long-Term Care Insurance System)*. <www.mhlw.go.jp/public/kekka/2010/dl/p0517-1a.pdf>

MHLW (2008a). *Heisei 18 nendo Kaigokyuufu jittaichousa houkoku (Report on the Payment of Long-Term Care Insurance's Benefit 2007)*. Health and Welfare Statistic Association, Tokyo.

MHLW (2008b). *Kaigo shokuin no youtuu tou kennkoumonndai ni kakawaru fukushi yougu riyou chousa (The Usage of Welfare Equipment on Care Worker's Health Issues Such as Back Pain)*. MHLW, Tokyo.

MHLW (2007). Heisei 18 nendo kaigo saabisu shisetsu/jigyousho chousa kekkano gaiyou (The research on long-term care providers 2007). <http://www.mhlw.go.jp/toukei/saikin/hw/kaigo/service06/kekka1.html>.

MHLW (2006a). *Chiiki micchakugata saasbisu niokeru jikohyouka oyobi gaibuhyou-kano jisshinituite (Request on the Self-Evaluation and Mandatory Thirdparty Evalu-ation for Community-Based Care Services)*. <www.mhlw.go.jp/shingi/2006/10/dl/s1005-7b01.pdf>

MHLW (2006b). Ninchi-shou koureisha Group Home riyou-sha futan (The users' expense of group home for elderly with dementia). *Asahi Newspaper*. <www.asahi.com/life/update/0312/001.html>

MHLW (2006c). *Shugyou hoken-shi, Josan-pu, kango-shi, jun-kango-shi (Public Health Nurse, Maternity Nurse, Certified Nurse, and Assistant Nurse on Duty)*. <www.mhlw.go.jp/toukei/saikin/hw/eisei/06/kekka1.htm>

MHLW (2002). *Long-Term Care Insurance in Japan*. <www.mhlw.go.jp/english/topics/elderly/care/index.html>

MHLW (2000). Social security systems throughout the world, annual reports on health and welfare 1998–1999. *Social Security and National Life, Vol. 2, White Paper.* MHLW, Tokyo.

MHLW (1996). *Jun-kangofu mondai chousa kentoukai houkoku no gaiyou (Summary of the Report on the Issue of Assistant Nurse).* MHLW, Tokyo.

MHLW (1995). *The Comprehensive Survey of the Living Conditions of People on Health and Welfare.* MHLW, Tokyo.

Milward, H. B. (1996). Symposium on the hollow state: Capacity, control, and performance in interorganizational setting. *Journal of Public Administration Research and Theory,* April: 193–314.

Milward, H. B. (1994). Implications of contracting out: New roles for the hollow state, in Ingraham, P., and Romzek, B. (eds), *New Paradigms for Government: Issues for the Changing Public Service.* Jossey-Bass, San Francisco.

Ministry of General Affairs (2006). Roudouryoku chosa nenpo (Labor force statistics), <http://www.stat.go.jp/data/roudou/report/2006/ft/index.htm>

Morozumi, R. (2007). Quality of care in Japanese group homes for the elderly with dementia: Synergy of facility services and medical services. *Working Paper No. 216.* Faculty of Economics, University of Toyama, Toyama.

Musgrave, R. (1959). *The Theory of Public Finance: A Study in Public Economy.* McGraw-Hill, London.

Musgrave, R. (1957). A multiple theory of budget determination. *Finanzarchiv,* Vol. 17 (3): 333–343.

Naegele, G. (2009). *15 Years Long-Term Care Insurance in Germany: Time for an Interim Evaluation: After the Reform Is before the (Next) Reform.* The 19th International Association of Gerontology and Geriatrics (IAGG) Congress 2009, July 5–9th, 2009, Paris.

Nanbu, T. (2000). Kaigo saabisu sangyo he no kotekikaigohoken donyu no keizaitekikiketsu (Economic consequences of introduction of public long-term care insurance system into long-term care industry in Japan), in National Institute of Population and Social Security Research (IPSS) (ed), *Iryo kaigo no sangyo bunseki (Analysis of Health Care and Long-Term Care Industry).* University Press, Tokyo.

NEDO (2010). *NEDO seika repouto 2010 (NEDO Outcome Report 2010).* <www.nedo.go.jp/kankobutsu/pamphlets/23seika/seika/index.html>

NEDO (2008). Ningen shien-gata robotto jitsuyouka kiban gijutsu kaihatsu (Developing the platform for the use of human support robot), in METI (ed), *21st Century Robot Challenge Program.* Ministry of Economics, Trade and Industry, Tokyo.

Niigata City (2014). *Kaigo hoken saabisu gaido (Long-Term Care Insurance Service Guide).* Niigata, Japan.

Niigata City (2008). *Kaigo hoken saabisu gaido (Long-Term Care Insurance Service Guide).* Niigata, Japan.

Nishimura, S. (2014). Kaigaini okeru fukushikokka kenyu no chouryu (The research trends of welfare states), in Nishimura, S., Kyogoku, T., and Kaneko, T. (eds), *shakaihoshou no kokusaihikaku kenkyu (International Comparative Research of Social Welfare).* Minerva shobo.

Nishimura, S., Kyogoku, T., and Kaneko, Y. (2014). *Shakaihosho koyoutoukei no riron to bunseki (Theory and Analysis on the Employment Statistics of Social Security).* Keio University Press.

Nissei Life Insurance Research Institute (1998). Oubei de susumu kaigo service he no shijou mechanism dounyuu (The introduction of market mechanism into elderly care services in Western nations: International comparison and the problem of Japan). *Nissei Kisokenkyu Report 1998*, February, NLI Research Institute, Tokyo.

Norton, E. C. (2017). Long-term care and pay-for-performance programs. *Review of Development Economics*, <https://doi.org/10.1111/rode.12359>

Norton, E. C. (2000). Long-term care, in Culyer, A. J., and Newhouse, J. P. (eds), *Handbook for Health Economics*, Vol. IB. Elsevier Science B. V., New York, 956–994.

Nyman, J. A. (1994). The effects of market concentration and excess demand on the price for nursing home care. *Journal of Industrial Economics*, Vol. 42 (2): 193–204.

Nyman, J. A. (1988). Excess-demand, the percentage of Medicaid patients, and the quality of nursing home care. *Journal of Human Resource*, Vol. 23 (1): 76–92.

Nyman, J. A. (1985). Prospective and cost-plus Medicaid reimbursement, excess Medicaid demand, and the quality of nursing home care. *Journal of Health Economics*, Vol. 4 (3): 237–259.

O'Brien, J., Saxberg, B. O., and Smith, H. L. (1983). For-profit or not-for-profit nursing homes: Does it matter? *Gerontologist*, Vol. 23: 341–348.

OECD (2009). *Population Statistics for OECD Member Countries*. OECD, Paris.

OECD (2005). *The OECD Health Report: Long-Term Care for Older People*. OECD, Paris.

OECD (2000). *The OECD Labour Force Statistics*. OECD, Paris.

Oshio, T. (2014). *Jizokukanou na shakaihoshou he (Towards a Sustainable Social Security)*. NTT Shuppan.

Oshio, T. (2013). *Shakaihosho no keizaigaku 4 (Economics of Social Security 4th Edition)*. Nihon hyoron sha.

Oshio, T. (2005). *Jinkou genshojidai no shakaihosho kaikaku (Social Security Reform in the Era of Population Decrease)*. Nihon keizai shinbunsha.

Ostrom, V. (1989). *The Intellectual Crisis in American Public Administration*. University of Alabama Press, Tuscaloosa, AL.

Ouslander, J. (1997). The resident assessment instrument: Promise and pitfalls. *Journal of the American Geriatrics Society*, Vol. 45: 975–976.

Paraprofessional Healthcare Institute (PHI) (2009). *Fact Sheet: Who Are Direct-Care Workers?* <http://nasuad.org/sites/nasuad/files/hcbs/files/152/7586/Direct_Care_Workers_factsheet.pdf>

Paraprofessional Healthcare Institute (PHI) (2008). *Health Coverage for Direct-Care Workers: 2008 Data Update*. <www.directcareclearinghouse.org/.../PHI-447%20FactSheet4_singles.pdf, December>, 2009.

Parkin, M., and Bade, R. (2006). Solution to odd-numbered problems, chapter 9 organization, production, economics, in *Canada in the Global Environment* (6th ed.). Pearson Education, Canada.

Peters, B. G., and Pierre, J. (1998). Governance without government? Rethinking public administration. *Journal of Public Administration Research and Theory*, Vol. 10: 35–48.

Phillips, C. D., *et al.* (1997). Association of the Resident Assessment Instrument (RAI) with changes in function, cognition, and psychosocial status. *Journal of the American Geriatrics Society*, Vol. 45: 986–993.

Rahman, A., and Applebaum, R. (2009). The nursing home minimum data set assessment instrument: Manifest functions and unintended consequences- past, present, and future. *The Gerontologist*, Vol. 49 (6): 727–735.

Robinson, J. C. (1988). Market structure, employment, and skill mix in the hospital industry. *Southern Economic Journal*, Vol. 55 (2): 315–325.

Robinson, J. C., and Luft, H. (1985). The impact of hospital market structure on patient volume, average length of stay, and cost of care. *Journal of Economics*, Vol. 3 (1): 1–24.

Robot Revolution Initiative (2017). *Home Page.* <www.jmfrri.gr.jp/index.html>

Sakurai, M. (2008). Hieiri/EIri soshikino saabisu no shitsu nikannsuru hikakukento (The comparison between for-profit and nonprofit in care service quality). *Journal of Research on NPOBP*, Vol. 10: 51–60.

Salamon, L. M. (1989). *Beyond Privatization: The Tools of Government Action.* Urban Institute Press, Washington, DC.

Sankai, Y. (2006). *Leading Edge of Cybernics: Robot Suit HAL, SICE-ICASE.* International Joint Conference, 18th–21st October, 2006, Busan, S. Korea.

Scanlon, W. J. (1980). A theory of the nursing home market. *Inquiry*, Vol. 17: 25–41.

Schmolling, P., Jr., Youkeles, M., and Burger, W. R. (1997). *Human Services in Contemporary America* (4th ed.). Brooks Cole Publishing, CA.

Schnelle, J. F. (1997). Can nursing homes use the MDS to improve quality? *Journal of the American Geriatrics Society*, Vol. 45: 1027–1028.

Schnelle, J. F., et al. (2003). The minimum data set urinary incontinence quality indicators: Do the reflect differences in care processes related to incontinence? *Medical Care*, Vol. 41: 909–922.

Seed Planning (2014). *Telepresensu robot to pawa ashisuto suitsu no saishin doukou (The Latest Update of Telepresence Robot and Power Assist Suit).* Sheed Plannning.

Selznick, P. (1949). *TVA and the Grass Roots.* University of California Press, Berkeley, CA.

Shimizutani, S., and Suzuki, W. (2002). The quality of efficiency of at-home long-term care in Japan: Evidence from micro-level data. *ESRI Discussion Paper Series* 18, Economic and Social Research Institute, Government of Japan.

Shimono, K., Otsu, H., and Okusa, Y. (2003). *Kaigo saabisu no keizaibunseki (Economic Analysis of Long-Term Care Services).* Toyo Keizai shinpo sha.

Shortell, S. M., and Hughes, E. F. (1988). The effect of regulation, competition, and ownership on mortality rates among hospital inpatients. *The New England Journal of Medicine*, Vol. 318: 1100–1107.

Simmons, S. F., et al. (2003). The minimum data set weight loss quality indicator: Does it reflect differences in care processes related to weight loss? *Journal of the American Geriatrics Society*, Vol. 51: 1410–1418.

Slevin, M. L., et al. (1998). Who should measure quality of life, the doctor or the patient? *British Journal of Cancer*, Vol. 57: 109–112.

Sloan, F. A., and Norton, E. C. (1997). Adverse selection, bequests, crowding out, and private demand for insurance: Evidence from the long-term care insurance market. *Journal of Risk and Uncertainty*, Vol. 15: 201–219.

Smith, S., and Lipsky, M. (1993). *Nonprofits for Hire: The Welfare State in the Age of Contracting.* Harvard University Press, Cambridge, MA.

Stiglitz, J. (2012). *The Price of Inequality.* W. W. Norton & Co. Inc.

Sturgess, G. (1996). Virtual government: What will remain inside the public sector? *Australian Journal of Public Administration*, Vol. 55 (3): 59–73.

Sugahara, T. (2010). Invited counter argument for managing the long-term care market: The constraints of service quality improvement. *Japanese Journal of Health Economics and Policy*, Vol. 21 (E1): 265.

Suzuki, W. (2002). Hierihoumon kaigosha wa yuri ka? (Do nonprofit care providers have advantages?). *Shakaihosho kenkyu*, Vol. 38 (1): 74–88.

Suzuki, W., and Satake, N. (2001). Nihon no kaigo saabisu jigyo no jittai (Analysing Japanese Care Service Industry). *Economics (Toyo Keizai Shinpo sha)*, Vol. 6: 180–195.

Tachibanaki, T. (2010). *Anshin no shakaihoshou kaikaku (Social Security Reform for Safety)*. Toyo Keizai shinpo sha.

Thomas, G. (2006). *Performance Measurement, Reporting, Obstacles and Accountability: Recent Trends and Future Directions*. ANU E Press. <http://epress.anu.edu.au/anzsog/performance/pdf/performance-whole.pdf>

Tokyo Metropolitan Foundation for Social Welfare and Public Health (2017). <www.fukushizaidan.jp>

Tuckman, H. P., and Chang, C. F. (1988). Cost convergence between for-profit and not-for-profit nursing homes: Does competition matter? *Quarterly Review of Economics and Business*, Vol. 28 (4): 50–65.

Tullock (1970). *Private Wants, Public Means*. Basic Books, New York.

Uman, G. (1997). Where's Gertrude? *Journal of the American Geriatrics Society*, Vol. 45: 1025–1026.

United Nations (2012). *World Population Prospects: The 2008 Revision Population Database*. <http://esa.un.org/unpp>

United Nations (2008). *World Population Prospects: The 2008 Revision Population Database*. <http://esa.un.org/unpp>

Vogel, E. F. (1979). *Japan as Number One: Lessons for America*. Harvard University Press, Cambridge, MA, USA.

Wada, K., Shibata, T., Musha, T., and Kimura, S. (2008). Robot therapy for elders affected by dementia: Using personal robots for pleasure and relaxation. *IEEE Engineering in Medicine and Biology Magazine*, July/August: 53–60.

Weisbrod, B. A. (1980). Heteroscedasticity-consistent covariance matrix estimator and a direct test for heteroscedasticity. *Econometorica*, Vol. 48 (4): 817–837.

Welfare and Medical Service Agency (2015). *Kaigoshokuin Shoninsha kensyu syuryosha (Early Career Care Workers)*. <www.wam.go.jp/content/wamnet/pcpub/top/fukushiworkguide/jobguidejobtype/jobguide_job06.html>

Welfare and Medical Service Agency (2010a). *Home Page*. <www.wam.go.jp>

Welfare and Medical Service Agency (2010b). *Kaigo-hoken seido kankei no kaigo jujisha no shikaku (Care Worker's Licenses of Long-Term Care Insurance System)*. <www.wam.go.jp/wamappl/bb05Kaig.nsf/0/41b148c659e3ac3849257759001e74fd/$FILE/20100707_1shiryou3_3.pdf>

Weller, P., Bakvis, H., and Rhodes, R. A. W. (1997). *The Hollow Crown: Countervailing Trends in Core Executives*. Macmillan Press Ltd., London.

Wholey, S. J., and Newcomer, E. K. (1997). Clarifying goals, reporting results, in Newcomer, E. K. (ed), *Using Performance Measurement to Improve Public and Non-Profit Programs: New Directions for Evaluation*. Jossey-Bass, San Francisco.

Wiener, J. M., *et al.* (2007). *Quality Assurance for Long-Term Care: The Experiences of England, Australia, Germany and Japan*. AARP, Washington, DC.

Wilmoth, J. R. (1998). The future of human longevity: A demographer's perspective. *Science*, Vol. 280: 395–397.

Wilson, J. C., and Jadlow, J. M. (1982). Competition, profit incentives, and technical efficiency in the provision of nuclear medicine services. *The Bell Journal of Economics*, Vol. 13: 472–482.

World Bank (2005). *World Development Indicators Database*. World Bank, Washington, DC.

Yamagishi, T. (2014). *America iryoseido no seijishi (Political History of US Medical Systems)*. The University of Nagoya Press, Nagoya.

Yano Research Institute (2013). *Kaigo robot no kanousei to shourai sei 2013 (The Possible Future of Care Robot 2013)*. Yano Research Institute.

Yin, R. (2002). *Applications of Case Study Research Second Edition (Applied Social Research Methods Series, Vol. 34)*. Sage Publications, Thousand Oaks, CA.

Zhou, Y., and Suzuki, W. (2004). Nihon no houmonkaigoshijo niokeru shijosyucyudo to kouritsusei (The correlation among the market centralization, efficiency and service quality in Japanese care market). *Japan Economic Research*, Vol. 49 (3): 173–187.

Zimmerman, D. R., *et al.* (1995). Development and testing of nursing home quality indicators. *Health Care Finance Review*, Vol. 16 (4): 107–127.

Zins, C. (2001). Defining human services. *Journal of Sociology and Social Welfare*, Vol. 28 (1): 3–21.

Zontek, T. L., Isernhagen, J. C., and Ogle, B. R. (2009). Psychosocial factors contributing to occupational injuries among direct care workers. *Official Journal of the American Association of Occupational Health Nurses*, Vol. 57 (8): 338–347.

Zwanziger, J., and Melnick, G. (1988). The effects of hospital competition and the Medicare PPS program on hospital cost behaviour in California. *Journal of Health Economics*, Vol. 7: 301–320.

Index